The Dark Side of Diplomacy

Unseen Forces Shaping Nations and Fates

By
B. K. Chaaraoui

Copyright 2024 B. K. Chaaraoui. All rights reserved.

No part of this book may be reproduced in any form or by any electronic or mechanical means including information storage and retrieval systems, without permission in writing from the author. The only exception is by a reviewer, who may quote short excerpts in a review.

Although the author and publisher have made every effort to ensure that the information in this book was correct at press time, the author and publisher do not assume and hereby disclaim any liability to any party for any loss, damage, or disruption caused by errors or omissions, whether such errors or omissions result from negligence, accident, or any other cause.

This publication is designed to provide accurate and authoritative information with regard to the subject matter covered. It is sold with the understanding that the publisher is not engaged in rendering professional services. If legal advice or other expert assistance is required, the services of a competent professional should be sought.

The fact that an organization or website is referred to in this work as a citation and/or a potential source of further information does not mean that the author or the publisher endorses the information the organization or website may provide or recommendations it may make.

Please remember that Internet websites listed in this work may have changed or disappeared between when this work was written and when it is read.

"To my father, on your 100th birthday, with all my love and gratitude."

Author Note

As I stare down from that mirror of the time in my dotage, I contemplate the history that could be written at present; as I catch glances of the turbulent times that have shaped the world in the past decades, there is so much undone, and there is a story to tell—my story twisted and twined so closely with the events through which the modern world was forged. I came into existence under the tumultuous skies of Lebanon at a time when history was enabling, and the collective echoes of global promises carried heightened undertones.

My childhood was punctuated by machine-gun fire and curfews during the 1958 revolution that rattled the sardine of a state called Lebanon. The war became the way of life since the Six-Day War of 1967 and the 1973 conflict. It took the brutal chaos of the Lebanese civil war and the Palestinian struggle to inflict my biggest scar, though, making sure society wouldn't heal for quite some time.

In this context and given the fictional urban reality we are interacting with, such a view should be political by definition. It was not that I became interested in politics; politics became a useful methodology for survival and a strange and fun fascination.

No, that was the maze of contention I had walked, its slender thread scrawling an atlas of politics and persuasion, the silent ballet of authority and force that bound realms.

My very brief brush with the enigmatic world of international affairs and political activism did give me a sense of practical experience to complement the theoretical learning I had acquired through academia.

Striving for transformation, á la Cadbury, versus Making A Difference, I was increasingly exposed to the corridors of richness that had me meandering through complexities and contradictions.

Regardless, let this booklet be not about me but a testament to the power of those who want to learn about the world outside of their walls. As much as I have weathered the storms of change and crossed the streams of policy and strategy, utilitarian political power is ultimately less victorious than the knowing but practical application of power.

The shades of our world were the same, fully painted with the abovementioned silence of diplomats tinting everywhere humankind passed through. Yet when we see the still ongoing hellfire of suffering, penetrating to the bone marrow of the oppressed people of Palestine, the question that haunts me is Have we gone so astray? Have we lost our sense of compassion? By decoding the secrets within the tangled knots of our common humanity and interpreting the cryptic art of diplomacy, we may eventually find the keys to a global society with less conflict and more humanity.

We still have so much to learn, but the more corners we turn and roads we cross we edge a little closer to grasping the full picture of how our world, so vast and varied, truly operates.

Table of Contents

Author Note iv
Contents vi
Introduction: Unveiling the Dark Side of Diplomacy 1
Chapter 1: The Art and Craft of Modern Diplomacy 3
    The Evolution of Diplomatic Practices 4
    Diplomacy's Dark Arts 7
    Espionage in Statecraft 8
    Recruiting Assets Abroad 8
    The Grand Chessboard of Diplomacy: Personal Cases of
    Manipulation and Betrayal 12
    The Provocateur. 13
    Disinformation: Warfare of Words 16
    From Secret Treaties to Public Agreements 28
    The Role of Non-State Actors 30
Chapter 2: The Tools of Influence and Manipulation 34
    Economic Levers and Sanctions 35
    The Power of Information Warfare 38
Chapter 3: Economic Hit Man and Sovereign Subjugation 41
    Debt 42
    Development 45
    Case Study: Dominance The Politics of Loans and Bailouts 47
Chapter 4: Behind Closed Doors: The Reality of
Diplomatic Intrigue 51

Case Studies of Notable Diplomatic Maneuvers 51
  Strategies of Covert Influence 54

Chapter 5: The Ethics of Diplomacy: Justifiable Pressure or Exploitation? 58
  The Line Between Persuasion and Coercion.................................. 58
  International Responses and Regulations 61

Chapter 6: The Shadows Over Resource Wars................................... 65
  The Hidden Battle for Energy and Minerals 66
  The Plight of Weaker Nations... 68

Chapter 7: Regional Tensions and the New Multipolar World 72
  Shifting Alliances and Power Balances.. 72
  The Impact on Global Governance 75

Chapter 8: Proxy Wars and Their Global Impact............................... 79
  Understanding the Proxy Wars in Ukraine and the Middle East ... 80
  Africa's Struggle within the International Chessboard.................. 83

Chapter 9: The Clandestine Operations to Gain Regional Dominance 87
  Case Studies on Covert Interventions... 88
  Covert Ops Chronicle 91
  Operation Ajax (1953, Iran).. 91
  Operation PBSUCCESS 1954, Guatemala 92
  The Congo Crisis (1960).. 92
  Operation Condor and South America in the 1970s..................... 93
  Operation Cyclone (1979-1989, Afghanistan)............................... 93
  The Iran-Contra Affair, 1980s, Nicaragua 94
  The Invasion Of Iraq (2003) 94
  Timber Sycamore 2012–2017... 94
  Legacy 95
  Long-Term Effects on Global Politics... 95

Chapter 10: The Influence of Non-Governmental Organizations (NGOs) and Multinational Corporations (MNCs) 99
    NGOs: From Humanitarian Aid to Political Influence 100
    MNCs and Their Role in Shaping Foreign Policy 103

Chapter 11: Cyber Diplomacy and Information Warfare 107
    The Emerging Battlefield: Cyberspace 108
    Strategies and Defenses Against Cyber Manipulation 110

Chapter 12: Moving Forward: Diplomacy in the 21st Century 114
    Innovations in Diplomatic Strategy 114
    Addressing the Challenges of a Connected World 117

Chapter 13: Shaping a More Transparent Future for Diplomacy 121

Appendix 125
    Historical Dark Side of Diplomacy 125
    Why This Matters 128
    Further Reading and Resources 128
    A Final Note 128

Glossary of Terms 130

List of Acronyms 133
    Recommended Resources 134

Introduction: Unveiling the Dark Side of Diplomacy

Ever wonder what lurks behind the polished smiles and firm handshakes that define the world stage? Well, you're about to dive into the murky waters where the swans of diplomacy paddle furiously below. It's a realm where the glow of the public eye barely reaches, and the rules of the game are, just say, flexibly interpreted. This isn't your high school history textbook's take on international relations. Nope, this is about peeling back the layers of the onion, tears and all, to reveal what the power brokers would rather keep hidden.

Sure, diplomacy might conjure images of stately figures debating over ornate tables, but the reality is more akin to a poker game where everyone's bluffing and the stakes are entire nations. From economic sanctions masquerading as persuasive tools to covert operations aimed at toppling regimes, it's a world where might often trumps right. We'll take you through the shadowy corridors of power, where influence is currency and the currency is, well, actual currency. It's a trip that'll reveal the maneuvers and machinations that shape the headlines and, occasionally, the borders of the world map.

So gear up for a jaunt through the less-than-savory aspects of global diplomacy. We're talking about everything from backdoor deals brokered in hushed tones to the high-tech battleground of cyber espionage. And while our journey might not always be comfortable, it promises to be enlightening. By understanding the undercurrents that steer the ship of state, we'll not only shed light on the dark corners of diplomacy but also equip ourselves with the knowledge to foresee, and maybe even influence, the currents yet to come. Welcome to the dark side; it's going to be an intriguing ride.

Chapter 1:
The Art and Craft of Modern Diplomacy

After peeling back the initial layers of diplomacy's ostensibly genteel veneer in the introduction, it's about time we dive headfirst into the frenzied, yet calculated world of modern diplomacy. This realm isn't just about the polished shoes and pressed suits navigating the glossy corridors of power; it's an intricate ballet, where each pirouette and plié must be performed with the precision of a seasoned artist. At its core, diplomacy today is a creative blend of old-school charm and high-stakes strategy, mingled with the latest digital tactics. We're not just talking about clinking glasses at state dinners anymore. Oh no, we're knee-deep in a 21st-century saga where every tweet, handshake, and unassuming USB drive can tilt the global balance of power. The evolution from smoke-filled rooms to encrypted chat rooms hasn't made the diplomatic dance any simpler. If anything, the inclusion of non-state actors and the transition from covert operations to strategies aired on the evening news have turned the diplomatic rulebook into something closer to a choose-your-own-adventure novel. And in reality, navigating this complex landscape requires more than just a good poker face; it demands an understanding of the nuances that drive public agreements and the subtleties that define the role of unconventional players on this global chessboard. So as we delve into the art and craft that underpin modern diplomacy, remember that this isn't your grandmother's tutorial on table manners at international summits. Rather, imagine we're sketching the blueprint for understanding how appearances often disguise the machinations of power and how today's diplomatic artisans weave their craft in a world that's always one tweet away from upheaval.

The Evolution of Diplomatic Practices

In certain reigns, in the dimly lit corridors of power, diplomacy was as much an art as it was a dark craft. If you've ever wondered how we've journeyed from clandestine meetings in shadowy back rooms to the hashtag diplomacy of today's digital age, you're in for quite the tale. It's a saga that highlights how diplomatic practices have undergone a significant transformation, reflecting broader changes in global power dynamics, technology, and public scrutiny.

In the days of kingdoms and empires, diplomacy was often a matter of life and death. Envoys and diplomats were the messengers between kings and emperors, carrying offers of alliances, threats of war, or the occasional marriage proposal to seal a deal. These individuals had to be skilled in the art of persuasion, fluent in several languages, and above all, expert keepers of secrets. Think of them as the original "cloak and dagger" operatives, minus the cool spy gadgets we fantasize about today.

Fast forward a few centuries, and by the time we hit the Renaissance, diplomacy started to get its own rulebook—literally. The establishment of resident embassies and the recognition of diplomatic immunity meant that those engaging in the art of negotiation could do so with a bit of a safety net. However, we shouldn't kid ourselves into thinking it was all genteel and respectful—espionage and intrigue were very much part of the diplomatic DNA.

Now leap to the 19th and early 20th centuries, and you hit the era of grand conferences and high-stakes diplomatic maneuvering. The Congress of Vienna, the Treaty of Versailles—these were the blockbusters of international diplomacy, setting the stage for modern international relations. Yet even with more formalized procedures and protocols, diplomacy remained a realm dominated by secrecy and backroom deals.

The Cold War era brought with it a sort of diplomatic duality. On one hand, public posturing and ideological battles played out on the world stage. On the other were covert operations, spy exchanges, and a hotline between the White House and the Kremlin that symbolized the ultimate direct line of communication—albeit one hoped never to be used. It was a time of paradoxes, of mutually assured destruction serving as peacekeeper, and of space races doubling as displays of technological prowess and diplomatic bargaining chips.

Come the late 20th and early 21st centuries, and the landscape shifts once more. The fall of the Berlin Wall and the dissolution of the Soviet Union unleashed a new world order, where unilateral power was momentarily unchallenged and diplomacy began to pivot toward addressing global issues like climate change, terrorism, and cyber security. The way countries communicated and worked together (or didn't, as the case often was) had to adjust to this new reality.

And it's important not to overlook the advent of the Internet and social media. Suddenly, diplomacy wasn't just happening in oak-paneled rooms among men in suits; it was happening on Twitter, Facebook, and WhatsApp. "Digital diplomacy" and "hashtag diplomacy" became the new buzzwords, signaling a shift toward more open, accessible discussions on foreign policy matters. Of course, whether a tweet can replace a handshake is a debate for another day, but the change in mediums is undeniable.

Along with the technological revolution came a push for transparency and accountability. The WikiLeaks saga and the revelations by whistleblowers like Edward Snowden threw a spotlight on the murky depths of diplomatic communications and espionage, forcing a conversation on privacy, surveillance, and the ethical boundaries of statecraft.

Today's diplomatic practices are thus a complex tapestry woven from the threads of history, technology, and evolving global challenges. We've seen a move toward multilateralism, with international organizations playing a more prominent role in facilitating dialogue and conflict resolution. Yet the effectiveness and legitimacy of these bodies are constantly under scrutiny, reflecting a broader debate on sovereignty and global governance.

Non-state actors, too, have emerged as significant players on the diplomatic stage. From multinational corporations to non-governmental organizations, these entities wield considerable influence, often shaping policy and public opinion just as powerfully as any state.

Environmental diplomacy has become a key focus area with climate change negotiations taking center stage in international forums. The art of diplomacy in this realm requires not just skillful negotiation but a deep understanding of science, economics, and the often-competing priorities of developed and developing nations.

And yet, despite all these changes, some things remain remarkably consistent. The core principles of diplomacy—negotiation, representation, and communication—are as relevant today as they were hundreds of years ago. Yes, the tools and tactics may have evolved, but the goal of advancing one's national interest while maintaining international peace and security persists.

So what can we make of this evolution? For starters, it's clear that diplomacy can't be confined to a static definition. It's adaptive, evolving in response to technological advancements, shifts in power dynamics, and global challenges. It's also increasingly public, with citizens around the world engaging in debates on foreign policy issues directly with their leaders and diplomats.

Does this mean we're entering an era of "diplomacy of the people, by the people, for the people"? Perhaps that's a bit optimistic, given the enduring influence of power politics. But there's no denying that the curtain has been pulled back, offering a glimpse into a world that was once shrouded in secrecy.

In wrapping up this journey through the evolution of diplomatic practices, it's worth pondering the future. With AI, virtual reality, and yet-undeveloped technologies on the horizon, the face of diplomacy is bound to change even more radically. Whether these changes make for a more peaceful and cooperative world or lead us down a more dystopian path remains to be seen. But one thing's for certain—it's going to be an interesting ride.

Ultimately, while the essence of diplomacy—managing the complex web of international relations with tact, negotiation, and strategic foresight—remains unchanged, the methods, tools, and actors are in constant flux. Navigating this ever-changing landscape requires not just a keen understanding of the past but also an imaginative grasp of the future. So stay vigilant and remain receptive; the next chapter in the story of diplomacy is being written as we speak.

Diplomacy's Dark Arts

Turning the lights on what's often dubbed 'diplomacy's dark arts,' we find a stage where the actors are skilled in more than just pleasant handshakes and formal dinners. It's a realm where shadows flit and whispers carry more weight than a public pronouncement. Within the labyrinth of international politics, espionage—we're talking crafty spooks and seductive moles—doesn't just thrive; it's an open secret doubling as an arms race, only with more tailored suits and less firepower (usually). It's clear as day that behind the façade of every embassy lies a backroom where smiles are forced and information is treated like gold or uranium, especially for the James Bond enthusiasts among us. Disinformation, on the other hand, is the warfare of words where reality is often the first casualty. It's where narratives are weaponized, and the truth is tailored like a bespoke suit to fit the occasion. They say knowledge is power, so it stands to reason that shaping what others perceive as truth wields a silent baton over the global power symphony. This chapter isn't just a dive deep into the rabbit hole; it's an exploration of the unspoken vernacular of geopolitics, doled out in deceptive whispers and cyber smokescreens. It's crucial to recognize that while it's easy to villainize these practices, understanding them is key to demystifying the complex machinations that keep the wheels of world powers turning.

Espionage in Statecraft

Peering through the looking glass of statecraft, it's no shocker that espionage serves up a piping-hot dish of intrigue and strategic advantage. Countries don't just idly stand by—spooks and secret agents are deployed with cloak-and-dagger finesse to garner the juiciest of secrets. Imagine, if you will, a grand chessboard where every move is shadowed by the ghostly whispers of the intelligence community. The irony, of course, is that while diplomacy smiles and shakes hands in the front room, espionage slinks through the back door, collecting the shredded clues and intelligence breadcrumbs that can pivot the course of history. It's an open secret that allies spy on foes, and shocker, even on each other! So as we explore the murky waters of state surveillance and clandestine ops, brace yourself for a narrative that's part James Bond, part George Smiley, but altogether a fundamental piece of the geopolitical puzzle we call the Great Game.

Recruiting Assets Abroad

Surprisingly, the often overlooked heroes and villains of global espionage are assets. They're the crucial cogs in the ever-whirring machine of global information gathering. You might think recruiting assets is a game played in dimly lit back allies with trench coats and fedoras—as classic as a black-and-white film—but hold on to your imagination; it's both more nuanced and far messier than that. In the world of diplomacy's hidden maneuvers, finding and turning assets abroad is an art form painted in shades of moral gray.

To understand the process, it's essential to know who these assets are. They can range from high-profile government officials with access to state secrets down to the unassuming local clerks who overhear tidbits of gold dust. It's all about their position, access, and willingness (or vulnerability) to spill the beans. More often than not, it's not a case of 'Will they, won't they?' but rather 'How can we make it worth their while?'

The motivations behind why individuals transform into assets are as varied as a spy novel's cast. Money is the old reliable motivator—everyone's got bills, right? But then you get the ideologues, the fervent believers in a cause willing to trade secrets for what they see as a greater good. Don't forget the disgruntled, those feeling slighted by their nation, looking for revenge or asserting control over their own lives. And sometimes, it's just about the thrill, the excitement of living a double life where every message could be the most crucial information one has ever laid hands on.

Now a golden rule in recruiting assets is 'patience is a virtue.' This isn't a wham-bam-thank-you-ma'am scenario; we're talking about an intricate dance, a subtle courtship. Intelligence officers must build relationships, assess vulnerabilities, and then, delicately, nudge their marks toward cooperation. Sometimes it's a soft touch—a shared interest here, an empathetic nod there—until trust blossoms into treachery against one's homeland. Crafting a false sense of security is part of the game, too. Covert operators have to be masterful actors and listeners. They find out what keeps their targets up at night and become the solution to those late-hour worries. This could mean offering up financial stability, protection for their family, or a stairway to a noble cause. It's about dangling the perfect carrot to keep those assets happy and chatty.

Recruiting isn't without risks, though. There's always the chance of a double-cross. Maybe the asset decides they're playing for the wrong team, or worse, they were a plant all along. It's a high-stakes game of chess with people as pawns, and sometimes you're unsure who's the king or queen until the game's almost over. These intelligence officers have to keep their wits sharp and their suspicions sharper to avoid being played for a fool.

Successful recruitment calls for leveraging local customs, too. It's one thing to understand the culture—it's another to inhabit it convincingly. It's like knowing the lyrics to a song versus singing it in perfect pitch. An intelligence officer living abroad must blend in, adopt local habits, and respect nuances in etiquette to gain genuine trust.

Technology—the wily beast. In today's world, a smartphone encrypts secrets and betrayals, with everyone from Moscow to Mongolia acutely aware of the digital footprint risks. Managing clandestine communications has become a minefield, with new encryption tools cropping up like moles in an arcade game. One wrong step, and boom, your asset's cover (and yours) is blown to smithereens.

Training assets ain't a stroll in the park either. They're often regular Joes and Janes, not trained spies. Cue the subtle art of teaching spycraft—how to notice tails, encrypt messages, and drop intel without dropping their cover. Juggling their day jobs with spy games can be mental gymnastics they may not have signed up for. It's like a secret part-time gig that could get them imprisoned—or worse—while publicly working nine-to-five in an office.

But don't think it's all about clandestine meetings and dead drops. These days, social engineering happens in chat rooms, forums, and online communities. The World Wide Web has become the Wild West of asset recruitment, replete with avatars instead of disguises, and connection speeds matter more than physical prowess.

For any nation playing the long game, recruiting assets abroad is investing in the future. It's about planting seeds in a garden you might not live to see but know one day will bear fruit for your homeland. Sure, it's a paradox, walking a line between patriotism and what might look an awful lot like treason from the other side.

In the world powers' endless chess match, assets given the right push can transform from pawns to queens, flipping the board entirely. It's a subtle acknowledgment that, while militaries hold the guns, information is the real ammunition used to win wars without firing a single shot. Now while your everyday Joe might slink into this espionage thriller with dreams of being 007, the truth is that for most assets, the story's less glamorous and much more perilous. Many live under the constant shadow of exposure, trading their normalcy for a sip of the adrenaline cocktail that is the intelligence game.

So there you have it, the uncut truth behind recruiting assets abroad. It's a game of human chess where emotions, loyalties, and lives are intertwined. Is it dirty work? Sure. Necessary? Ask any world power, and they'll say yes without a hint of irony. Diplomacy's dark arts require agents to pull on any number of heartstrings and purse strings, and often, no string is left untagged to defend the interests of the homeland.

The chessboard's set, the players ready, and in the end, it's all about keeping your allies close and your assets closer. It's an intricate tap dance on the global stage, and each slip-up can score a win for the other side or send the whole thing toppling down. Rest assured, tomorrow's headlines might just be shaped by the shadowy work done under today's cover of darkness.

B. K. Chaaraoui

The Grand Chessboard of Diplomacy: Personal Cases of Manipulation and Betrayal

From the strategic manipulations on the global stage—described in the preceding pages—we turn to the personal story of Barbour, illustrating the profound impact of these international games on individual lives. His journey into the world of political intrigue and espionage exemplifies how the grand chessboard of global diplomacy affects people on a personal level. Caught within the web of deceit orchestrated by nations, Barbour's initiation into the dark arts of diplomacy showcases how individuals are often unwittingly drawn into the complex machinery of foreign affairs. Their loyalty and emotions are manipulated for purposes beyond their comprehension at that moment. This shift from the abstract to the personal underscores the intricate and perilous nature of being an asset for a foreign power, fraught with dangers and moral ambiguity.

The art of recruiting foreign assets or informants goes beyond mere diplomacy, often involving the cunning enlistment of citizens to advance foreign interests under the guise of internal politics. This elaborate deception can take years to orchestrate and, sadly, often ends in heartbreaking betrayal and backstabbing, as demonstrated by the case of Mole Within. While being an asset for a foreign power might seem like a dream job, nothing could be further from the truth. This world is not only about high-stakes and dangerous missions—spying, passing information, sabotage, instigation, assassinations, or sowing division to keep conflicts alive—but also about being a traitor.

Recruiting agents and informants for foreign interests is much like assembling a team of spies, akin to being caught in a 007 film. It involves people from all backgrounds, including those in high political positions. As it turned out, just when we were doing more research on the matter, a certain smoking gun was set off by the Canada Spy Agency. Yet in a high-stakes espionage game, Canada became the center of that game today. In a bombshell report, Canadian intelligence had alerted the government of an alarming trend: a staggering number of serving and ex-members of Parliament are collaborating with foreign governments and are involved in criminal activities or worse, perhaps.

A prominent political leader summed up the revelation, stating, "I am more convinced than ever of the conclusions of the NSICOP committee and the report, that some parliamentarians are willing participants in the efforts of foreign states to interfere in our politics," adding that those involved are "traitors to the country."

As the Canadian saga is still fresh off the press and most likely to be swept under the rug until the truth seeps out, if it ever does, the focus in the pages that follow will bring to light some anecdotal reflections on the lambs that are led to the slaughter—ordinary individuals who inadvertently stumble into the exciting but hazardous world of espionage.

The Provocateur.

In 1970, the wheels of fate began to turn for a young Barbour. Sequestered within the confines of his home for reasons best left unspoken, Barbour's father saw in him a trusted courier for a massage destined for the leader of a formidable political and militant organization. What seemed like a simple task would soon become the opening act of Barbour's entanglement with shadowy realms of power. The young lad, eager and unsuspecting, had no inkling that this mission would ignite a passion within him, setting the stage for a lifelong dance with the darker side of politics.

Shortly after he arrived, he was in a large meeting room speaking with the politician himself when, unexpectedly, two men entered the room. They looked like they had a military background, and what he heard was a disturbing exchange of words. More disturbingly, neither of them told him to leave the room with a gesture inviting him to sit still. Barbour was about to learn what foreign operatives do. The men came back to the room with a man in handcuffs. He looked to be in his early forties, decently dressed but distraught. In a short time, the man began to spill his beans and tell who his handlers were. He was classified as an agitator-supposed to attend a religious gathering and participate in ritual activities but was tasked with reciting a prepared seditious slogan. He said he would do anything for a dollar, and for this mission, he was paid ten large, $10,000! Ten thousand dollars could buy you a house then. Once the interrogation ended, he was handed over to the proper authorities—at least that is what Barbour thought. Only as the years went by did he realize that serving as the local branch of a spook factory is more than just action and speaking well. It demanded boldness and articulacy, as well as the unwavering commitment to the cause that can disrupt the whole structure of a group or even plunge the whole country into darkness. It is a dangerous game, but someone has to play it.

As it happened, Barbour had a very close friend, "M," whom I will introduce on the next page: "A Mole Within" who played the game well.

A Mole Within: The Disillusionment in Beirut—Betrayal, ideology, and manipulation of a political prodigy.

They were four student rebels in the politically roiled suburbs of Beirut, where allegiances and ideologies swayed like the cedar trees in the mountain winds: Marco, Khal, Amir, and Barbour were known collectively as M.K.A.B. They epitomized the very essence of camaraderie and idealism. They were a close-knit brotherhood bound by common dreams and dedication to the plight of the working class. Each played his role, but it was M who was the political brain, the charismatic leader who left an indelible mark on the group and on the political landscape that was to follow. M was not only a friend; he was a shaper of thought, a sculptor of the minds of youth, those young minds craving for a difference, and he fed it. Over the growing years, with the influence of M's eloquent discourse, these young idealists were molded into crusading socialists. They believed, unequivocally, that they were fighting for justice, equality, and the underdog. The political atmosphere around them was one of instability and unpredictability, befitting a region always on the brink of change or disaster. This was the region in which M's skills shone at their best, steadying choppy waters like a mariner of long experience. The narrative, quite dramatically, turned upside down during a crucial political moment. There he was, right at the top of a powerful association as president, on that stage where the light was bright and the shadows lengthy across the boards. What was to ensue was a veritable political earthquake. In one moment, with the world as his witness, M declared a shocking change of loyalties, from the far left to the extreme right, in a pivot that left many of his comrades and audience in disbelief.

The ideological chasm was too wide to bridge; M had not just crossed over, he had obliterated his former self. In the minds of many, it was tantamount to betrayal and selling the soul to the dark and most sinister interests. The fallout was immediate and severe. M, once the beloved leader and influencer, became a persona non grata, a pariah within his circle. Theories abounded. Had he been manipulated? Was his radical shift the result of external pressures or perhaps an enticement from powerful entities with agendas of their own? The group he once led with such fervor splintered irreparably. K, A, and B found their paths diverging wildly in the wake of M's defection. Mr. K channeled his disillusionment in the world of political journalism, finally emerging as editor of a great magazine. Mr. A turned toward the law, becoming a respected litigator, professor, and defender of civil liberties. In the meantime, caught between two worlds, Mr. B. negotiated the political and commercial swamps, and his faith in ideological purity darkened. M's journey continued far from Lebanese soil. After a narrow escape from what could have been a deadly consequence of the event, he sought refuge in a foreign land. There, M entered the political arena once again, but his past clung to him like a shadow. Despite serving a lifetime as a politician and a diplomat, his career was marred by controversy and disgrace, a testament to the inescapable reach of one's political misdeeds. It is a moving story of M and his friends, revealing how fragile political beliefs are and how easily they can be ma-nipulated by external forces. In places like Beirut, where the political make-up is as unstable as the history that forms it, the distinction be-tween true ideological loyalty and opportunism becomes increasingly blurred, rendering even the most stalwart of individuals potential vic-tims of pressure and manipulation. The cautionary tale of M.K.A.B. echoes through the halls of power and through the coffee shops and meeting rooms where the next generation of political minds is being wrought. This is a cautionary tale of the price of betrayal and the very dangerous, often perilous dance of ideology and power. Then, a year later, Lebanon plunged into a catastrophic civil war that lasted for years, with its aftermath still felt today.

Disinformation: Warfare of Words

In the shadowy corridors of global politics, where the twang of clandestine meetings often gets deafening, a subtler, perhaps more insidious tool of power slinks through the airwaves and fiberoptics: disinformation. Oh yeah, the art of warfare isn't just about drones and SEAL teams; sometimes, it's all about the perfect mirage and phantom served not in a desert storm but over the endless expanse of the Inter-net— cue in the 'Warfare of Words.'

There's no denying it—the idea of twisting the truth, molding it like warm mozzarella until it barely resembles reality, has been in-grained in human history for ages. But in an age when a tweet can trig-ger a stock market crash or a deepfake can paint the Mona Lisa with a mustache and make you believe it's an undiscovered Da Vinci, we're playing a whole new ball game.

The Dark Side of Diplomacy

Imagine this scenario. Picture a room—no, not dark and smoke-filled, that's too cliché. Think modern, and sleek, with an ominous glow emanating from a wall of screens. The suits in that room—are they government officials? Crafty political strategists? No. These are the keyboard warriors, the digital ninjas launching payloads of carefully worded falsehoods, each syllable calculated to disrupt, divide and conquer.

But wait, before we get ahead of ourselves with visions of cyberpunk dystopias, consider the why. Why would a state, or non-state actor for that matter, choose to engage in this less bombastic, though equally devastating form of sparring? Simple—it's about influence. It's about shaping perceptions to such a degree that reality becomes a matter of opinion, not fact. Influencing elections? Been there, done that. How about nudging a referendum? Brexit bells ring a bell? Or merely sowing discord among a population to weaken the societal fabric? Piece of cake, mate. This isn't just about causing momentary chaos; it's about long-term shifts in the geopolitical landscape, and it starts with a kernel of doubt—subtly implanted, carefully nurtured until it grows into a forest of uncertainty.

It's not all existential threats and Bond villain schemes, though. Consider disinformation as the Swiss Army knife in the spy's pocket. Need to discredit a dissident? Spread a scandalous—albeit false—rumor. Want to pivot from a policy flop? Leak some alternative facts to muddy the waters. The possibilities are as endless as the depths of human gullibility.

What's truly insidious about disinformation is its chameleon-like ability to blend into our daily feed. Dressed up as memes, clickbait articles, or inflammatory social media posts, it lurks in plain sight, waiting to be shared, liked, and believed. And no one's immune. Not the earnest grad student researching for their thesis, not the stay-at-home parent scrolling through the news while on a coffee break, not even the seasoned journalist. The algorithms know what we like, what stokes our passions, and they deliver—straight to our digital doorstep—a steady diet of reality-lite.

World leaders aren't just prepping for NATO summits or G7 meetings; they're carefully crafting narratives, or counternarratives, testing the waters of public opinion with half-truths or outright fabrications. Suddenly, their opponents aren't just political adversaries—they're agents of chaos, purveyors of fake news.

Still, it's crucial not to tar everyone with the same brush. There are those in the intel community and media who fight the valiant fight for truth. Fact-checkers, investigative journalists, and whistle-blowers—they're the unsung heroes in this drama. Yet the tidal wave of misinformation they face can feel like fighting a hydra: Cut off one head, and two more emerge.

At the heart of this struggle is the weaponization of information. In days long gone, libraries burnt and presses smashed signified the suppression of knowledge. Today, too many truths clutter the field, each vying for the title of reality, and amidst this cacophony, the genuine article often becomes a mere whisper, drowned out by the shouts of persuasive lies.

So what's the defense against this onslaught? It's not as simple as installing a firewall or updating your antivirus—though a healthy dose of digital literacy surely wouldn't hurt. The real antidote to disinformation might just be a return to critical thinking, to questioning more than just accepting, to finding merit in doubt—constructive doubt, that is.

And perhaps a touch of empathy could go a long way. The understanding that behind every screen is a person with hopes, fears, and the capacity to be led astray could foster a more discerning approach to what we view and share. In a landscape where the battle for hearts and minds can turn friends into foes with a single well-placed lie, kindness in our discourse could be our saving grace.

But we shouldn't fool ourselves. It's a tall order in a world that often rewards speed over scrutiny and sensationalism over substance. Yet the cost of yielding to the convenience of pre-packaged narratives is too high. In the warp and woof of geopolitical gamesmanship, truth's fabric is the first to fray.

Closing this Pandora's box of disinformation once opened will be no mean feat. But understanding how the 'Warfare of Words' permeates our global discourse is a vital step. Being aware of the dark arts of diplomacy doesn't just reveal the wizard behind the curtain—it also equips us to confront the illusions and, maybe, just maybe, reclaim a bit of that elusive.

Weaponizing Disinformation. Confession of a Spy.

In his book By Way of Deception, Victor Ostrovesky tells what he had experienced in his life as a Mossad agent. His story, his words:

Revealing the facts as I know them from my vantage point of four years spent inside the Mossad was by no means an easy task.

Coming from an ardent Zionist background, I had been taught that the state of Israel was incapable of misconduct. That we were the David in the unending struggle against the ever-growing Goliath. That there was no one out there to protect us but ourselves—a feeling reinforced by the Holocaust survivors who lived among us.

We, the new generation of Israelites, the resurrected nation on its own land after more than two thousand years of exile, were entrusted with the fate of the nation as a whole.

The commanders of our army were called champions, not generals. Our leaders were captains at the helm of a great ship. I was elated when

I was chosen and granted the privilege to join what I considered to be the elite team of the Mossad.

But it was the twisted ideals and self-centered pragmatism that I encountered inside the Mossad, coupled with this so-called team's greed, lust, and total lack of respect for human life, that motivated me to tell this story.

It is out of love for Israel as a free and just country that I am laying my life on the line by doing so, facing up to those who took it upon themselves to turn the Zionist dream into the present-day nightmare.

The Mossad, being the intelligence body entrusted with the responsibility of plotting the course for the leaders at the helm of the nation, has betrayed that trust. Plotting on its own behalf, and for petty, self-serving reasons, it has set the nation on a collision course with all-out war.

One of the main themes of this book is Victor's belief that Mossad is out of control, that even the prime minister, although ostensibly in charge, has no real authority over its actions ...

Victor Ostrovsky, a former Israeli Mossad agent, wrote two books about Israel's terror against their enemies. In one of them, he discusses the fate of Palestinians who illegally cross the border in search of work in Israel. Many thousands of these young men simply are never heard from again after being captured by Israel's forces. Some of them are taken to the ABC research facilities, where they endure the indescribable terror of chemical, nuclear or biological warfare. The Mossad—believe it or not—has just 30 to 35 case officers, or katsas, operating in the world at any one time. The main reason for this extraordinarily low total, as you will read in this book, is that, unlike other countries, Israel can tap the significant and loyal cadre of the worldwide Jewish community outside Israel. This is done through a unique system of sayanim, volunteer Jewish helpers.

The Dark Side of Diplomacy

My first six weeks were uneventful. I worked at the downtown office, essentially as a gofer and filing clerk. But one chilly day in February 1984, I found myself joining 14 others on a small bus. ... This course was to be known as Cadet 16, as it was the sixteenth course of Mossad cadets. He walked briskly to the head of the table while the other two sat at the back of the room. "My name is Aharon Sherf," he said. "I am the head of the Academy. Welcome to the Mossad. Its full name is Ha Mossad, le Modiyn ve le Tafkidim Mayuhadim" [the Institute for Intelligence and Special Operations].

Our motto is: 'By way of deception, thou shalt do war.'

"It's the old Trojan dick trick." He lit a cigarette.

"What's that?" I couldn't help smiling; I'd never heard it called that before.

"I knew that would get your attention," he said, grinning. "Shimon activated Operation Trojan in February of this year."

I nodded. I'd still been in the Mossad when that order was given, and because of my naval background and acquaintance with most of the commanders in the navy, I participated in the planning for the operation as liaison with the navy.

A Trojan was a special communication device that could be planted by naval commandos deep inside enemy territory. The device would act as a relay station for misleading transmissions made by the disinformation unit in the Mossad, called LAP, and intended to be received by American and British listening stations. Originating from an IDF navy ship out at sea, the prerecorded digital transmissions could be picked up only by the Trojan. The device would then rebroadcast the transmission on another frequency, one used for official business in the enemy country, at which point the transmission would finally be picked up by American ears in Britain. The listeners would have no doubt they had intercepted a genuine communication, hence the name

Trojan, reminiscent of the mythical Trojan horse. Further, the content of the messages, once deciphered, would confirm information from other intelligence sources, namely the Mossad. The only catch was that the Trojan itself would have to be located as close as possible to the normal origin of such transmissions because of the sophisticated methods of triangulation the Americans and others would use to verify the source.

In the particular operation Ephraim was referring to, two elite units in the military had been made responsible for the delivery of the Trojan device to the proper location. One was the Matkal reconnaissance unit, and the other was Flotilla 13, the naval commandos. The commandos were charged with the task of planting the Trojan device in Tripoli, Libya.

On the night of February 17-18, two Israeli missile boats, the SAAR 4-class Moledet, armed with Harpoon and Gabriel surface-to-surface missiles among other weaponry, and the Geula, a Hohit-class missile boat with a helicopter pad and regular SAAR 4-class armament, conducted what seemed like a routine patrol of the Mediterranean, heading for the Sicilian channel and passing just outside the territorial waters of Libya. Just north of Tripoli, the warships, which were visible to radar both in Tripoli and on the Italian island of Lampedusa, slowed down to about four knots—just long enough to allow a team of twelve naval commandos in four wet submarines nicknamed "pigs" and two low-profiled speedboats called "birds" to disembark. The pigs could carry two commandos each and all their fighting gear.

The birds, equipped with an MG 7.62-caliber machine gun mounted over the bow and an array of antitank shoulder-carried missiles, could facilitate six commandos each while towing the empty pigs. The birds brought the pigs as close to the shore as possible, thus cutting down the distance the pigs would have to travel on their own. (The pigs were submersible and silent but relatively slow.)

The Dark Side of Diplomacy

Two miles off the Libyan coast, the lights of Tripoli could be seen glistening in the southeast. Eight commandos slipped quietly into the pigs and headed for shore. The birds stayed behind at the rendezvous point, ready to take action should the situation arise. Once they reached the beach, the commandos left their cigar-like transporters submerged in the shallow water and headed inland, carrying a dark green Trojan cylinder six feet long and seven inches in diameter. It took two men to carry it.

A gray van was parked on the side of the road about one hundred feet from the water, on the coastal highway leading from Sabratah to Tripoli and on to Benghazi. There was hardly any traffic at that time of night. The driver of the van seemed to be repairing a flat tire. He stopped working as the team approached and opened the back doors of the van. He was a Mossad combatant. Without a word said, four of the men entered the van and headed for the city. The other four returned to the water, where they took a defensive position by the submerged pigs. Their job was to hold this position to ensure an escape route for the team now headed for the city.

At the same time, a squadron of Israeli fighters was refueling south of Crete, ready to assist. They were capable of keeping any ground forces away from the commandos, allowing them a not-so-clean getaway. At this point, the small commando unit was divided into three details—its most vulnerable state. Were any of the details to run into enemy forces, they were instructed to act with extreme prejudice before the enemy turned hostile.

The van parked at the back of an apartment building on Al Jamhuriyh Street in Tripoli, less than three blocks away from the Bab al Azizia barracks that were known to house Qadhafi's headquarters and residence. By then, the men in the van had changed into civilian clothing. Two stayed with the van as lookouts, and the other two helped the

Mossad combatant take the cylinder to the top floor of the five-story building. The cylinder was wrapped in a carpet.

In the apartment, the top section of the cylinder was opened, and a small dishlike antenna was unfolded and placed in front of the window facing north. The unit was activated, and the Trojan horse was in place.

The Mossad combatant had rented the apartment for six months and had paid the rent in advance. There was no reason for anyone except the combatant to enter the apartment. However, if someone should decide to do so, the Trojan would self-destruct, taking with it most of the upper part of the building. The three men headed back to the van and to their rendezvous with their friends on the beach.

After dropping the commandos at the beach, the combatant headed back for the city, where he would monitor the Trojan unit for the next few weeks. The commandos wasted no time and headed out to sea. They didn't want to be caught in Libyan waters at daybreak. They reached the birds and headed at full speed to a prearranged pickup coordinate, where they met with the missile boats that had brought them in.

By the end of March, the Americans were already intercepting messages broadcast by the Trojan, which was only activated during heavy communication traffic hours. Using the Trojan, the Mossad tried to make it appear that a long series of terrorist orders were being transmitted to various Libyan embassies around the world (or, as they were called by the Libyans, Peoples' Bureaus). As the Mossad had hoped, the transmissions were deciphered by the Americans and construed as ample proof that the Libyans were active sponsors of terrorism. What's more, the Americans pointed out, Mossad reports confirmed it.

The Dark Side of Diplomacy

The French and the Spanish, though, were not buying into the new stream of information. To them, it seemed suspicious that suddenly, out of the blue, the Libyans, who'd been extremely careful in the past, would start advertising their future actions. They also found it suspicious that in several instances, Mossad reports were worded similarly to coded Libyan communications.

They argued further that, had there truly been after-the-fact Libyan communications regarding the attack, then the terrorist attack on the La Belle discotheque in West Berlin on April 5 could have been prevented, since surely there would have been communications before, enabling intelligence agencies listening in to prevent it. Since the attack wasn't prevented, they reasoned that it must not be the Libyans who did it, and the "new communications" must be bogus. The French and the Spanish were right. The information was bogus, and the Mossad didn't have a clue who planted the bomb that killed one American serviceman and wounded several others. But the Mossad was tied in to many of the European terrorist organizations, and it was convinced that in the volatile atmosphere that had engulfed Europe, a bombing with an American victim was just a matter of time. Heads of the Mossad were counting on the American promise to retaliate with vengeance against any country that could be proven to support terrorism. The Trojan gave the Americans the proof they needed. The Mossad also plugged into the equation Qadhafi's lunatic image and momentous declarations, which were really only meant for internal consumption.

It must be remembered that Qadhafi had marked a line in the water at that time, closing off the Gulf of Sidra as Libyan territorial waters and calling the new maritime border the line of death (an action that didn't exactly give him a moderate image). Ultimately, the Americans fell for the Mossad ploy head over heels, dragging the British and the Germans somewhat reluctantly in with them. Operation Trojan was one of the Mossad's greatest successes. It brought about the air strike on Libya that President Reagan had promised—a strike that had three important consequences. First, it derailed a deal for the release of the American hostages in Lebanon, thus preserving the Hizballah (Party of God) as the number one enemy in the eyes of the West. Second, it sent a message to the entire Arab world, telling them exactly where the United States stood regarding the Arab-Israeli conflict. Third, it boosted the Mossad's image of itself, since it was they who, by ingenious sleight of hand, had prodded the United States to do what was right. It was only the French who didn't buy into the Mossad trick and were determined not to ally themselves with the aggressive American act. The French refused to allow the American bombers to fly over their territory on their way to attack Libya.

On April 14, 1986, one hundred and sixty American aircraft dropped over sixty tons of bombs on Libya. The attackers bombed Tripoli international airport, Bab al Azizia barracks, Sidi Bilal naval base, the city of Benghazi, and the Benine airfield outside Benghazi. The strike force consisted of two main bodies, one originating in England and the other from flattops in the Mediterranean. From England came twenty-four F-111s from Lakenheath, five EF-111s from Upper Heyford, and twenty-eight refueling tankers from Mildenhall and Fairford. In the attack, the air force F-111s and the EF-111s were joined by eighteen A-6 and A-7 strike and strike support aircraft, six F\A-18 fighters, fourteen EA-6B electronic jammer planes, and other support platforms. The navy planes were catapulted from the carriers Coral Sea and America. On the Libyan side, there were approximately forty civilian casualties, including Qadhafi's adopted daughter. On the American side, a pilot and his weapons officer were killed when their F-111 exploded.

After the bombing, the Hizballah broke off negotiations regarding the hostages they held in Beirut and executed three of them, including one American named Peter Kilburn. As for the French, they were rewarded for their nonparticipation in the attack by the release at the end of June of two French journalists held hostage in Beirut. (As it happened, a stray bomb hit the French embassy in Tripoli during the raid.)

Ephraim had spelled it all out for me and confirmed some of the information I'd already known. He then went on. "After the bombing of Libya, our friend Qadhafi is sure to stay out of the picture for some time. Iraq and Saddam Hussein are the next target. We're starting now to build him up as the big villain. It will take some time, but in the end, there's no doubt it'll work."

"But isn't Saddam regarded as moderate toward us, allied with Jordan, the big enemy of Iran and Syria?"

"Yes, that's why I'm opposed to this action. But that's the directive, and I must follow it. Hopefully, you and I will be done with our little operation before anything big happens. After all, we have already destroyed his nuclear facility, and we are making money by selling him technology and equipment through South Africa."

In the following weeks, more and more discoveries were made regarding the big gun and other elements of the Saddam war machine. The Mossad had all but saturated the intelligence field with information regarding the evil intentions of Saddam the Terrible, banking on the fact that before long, he'd have enough rope to hang himself. It was very clear what the Mossad's overall goal was. It wanted the West to do its bidding, just as the Americans had in Libya with the bombing of Qadhafi. After all, Israel didn't possess carriers and ample air power, and although it was capable of bombing a refugee camp in Tunis, that was not the same. The Mossad leaders knew that if they could make Saddam appear bad enough and a threat to the Gulf oil supply, of which he'd been the protector up to that point, then the United States and its allies would not let him get away with anything but would take measures that would all but eliminate his army and his weapons potential, especially if they were led to believe that this might just be their last chance before he went nuclear.

From Secret Treaties to Public Agreements

Some years ago, diplomacy was like an exclusive club where whispers turned into global tremors. But let's spill some tea here: That era of secret handshakes and smoke-filled rooms is fading into the backdrop of history. We're now in the age of public agreements, where a tweet can signal a policy shift and a press conference can replace undercover meetings—well, sort of.

The shift from cloak-and-dagger to transparent diplomacy isn't just about modern technology airing everyone's dirty laundry in real-time. It's a complex dance of public perception, international law, and the unquenchable human thirst for information.

Consider for a moment the notorious secret treaties of yesteryears, where nations carved up territories like Thanksgiving turkeys away from prying eyes. Fast forward to today, and you've got international agreements being live-streamed, with diplomats poised like rock stars at the podium. Yes, diplomacy has its own rock stars now—imagine that!

Realistically speaking, the transition hasn't been all rainbows and unicorns. The road from secret treaties to public agreements is littered with the carcasses of failed negotiations, leaked documents, and the occasional diplomatic faux pas that sends everyone scrambling.

Think about it: When diplomacy was a behind-the-scenes affair, negotiators could finagle and compromise without the harsh glare of the public eye. Now every word is dissected, and every decision is second-guessed by an army of armchair analysts. It's like playing poker with your cards facing out—terrifying, isn't it?

Yet, there's an undeniable allure to this newfound transparency. Public agreements create a sense of participation, a belief that we're all in this together, navigating the choppy waters of international relations on a ship built of livestreams and press releases.

And here's where the irony kicks in: while the process may seem more transparent, the art of diplomacy has become even more sophisticated. Today's diplomats must be part strategist, part showman, and part tightrope walker, always mindful of the public eye's omnipresent gaze.

One might argue that this shift has democratized diplomacy, bringing it into the public square for a communal dissection. Gone are the days when treaties were signed, sealed, and delivered without a single citizen's input. Nowadays, public opinion can shape, shift, and sometimes shatter diplomatic endeavors.

So what does this mean for the future of diplomacy? For starters, it demands a new breed of diplomats—ones adept with not just a pen and a handshake but also with social media and sound bites. It means that the ripple effects of diplomatic actions are felt faster and more broadly than ever before.

Despite the push for transparency, the shadows haven't completely dissipated. Secret negotiations still happen because sometimes, that's the only way to get things done. The difference is that now those secrets are harder to keep. In the digital age, leaks are the new normal, and confidentiality is a fragile veil.

It's a double-edged sword, this transparency business. On one hand, it heralds a new era of accountability and public engagement. On the other, it makes the diplomatic tightrope even thinner and more treacherous.

And then there's the issue of misinformation. In a world where agreements are dissected in real-time, the truth can sometimes get lost in translation—or worse, twisted to serve particular agendas. Navigating this landscape requires not just diplomatic skill but also a savvy understanding of media and public perception.

So, dear friends, we find ourselves at a crossroads in the art and craft of modern diplomacy. From secret treaties to public agreements, the journey has been nothing short of revolutionary. But as we look toward the horizon, one thing is clear: the world of diplomacy will continue to evolve, and so must those who inhabit it.

The modern diplomat must be a chameleon, changing colors with the shifting landscape of global politics. They must be as comfortable in the limelight as they are in the shadowy corners of negotiation rooms. It's a tall order, to be sure. But in this brave new world of public agreements, it's the only way to ensure that diplomacy continues to thrive.

And there you have it—a glimpse into the transformation of diplomacy from the clandestine maneuvers of yesterday to the public spectacles of today. As the curtain rises on this new era, one thing's for sure: The art of diplomacy has never been more critical—or more captivating.

The Role of Non-State Actors

In an age where the word 'diplomacy' conjures images of stuffy rooms and stiffer personalities, there's a plot twist. Non-state actors are crashing the party, and they're shaking things up, from multinational corporations (MNCs) wielding economic might to non-governmental organizations (NGOs) armed with moral authority. Strap in, because the traditional state-centric view of international relations is getting a run for its money.

First and foremost, we'll address those business behemoths, the MNCs. These entities operate on a scale that can match, and occasionally surpass, the GDP of certain nations. They're not just in the game for profit; they've got agendas that can influence policies and politics on a global scale. Think of them as the rich uncles of diplomacy: Their money talks, and it often says, "Do as I say, not as I do."

On the other end of the spectrum, we've got NGOs. These are the folks who've taken "be the change you want to see in the world" as a life mantra. Armed with nothing but sheer will and moral high grounds, they push for changes that most governments would balk at. They're like the David to the state's Goliath, proving that you don't need to wield economic power to bring about seismic shifts in policy and public opinion.

Then there are the rogues of the modern diplomatic tale: terrorist groups, insurgents, and other armed non-state actors. They're the wild cards, unpredictable and capable of tilting international relations on their head with a single act. While their methods are, to put it mildly, frowned upon, their impact on the art and craft of modern diplomacy is undeniable.

We can't forget the tech giants and their role as non-state actors. In an era where data is more valuable than oil, these companies command an astonishing level of influence over the flow of information. They can sway public opinion, influence electoral outcomes, and even become arbiters of truth, all without firing a shot. In the chess game of international politics, they're playing 4D chess while everyone else is stuck on checkers.

What's particularly fascinating is how these non-state actors are not just participants but are shaping the rules of the game. They're lobbying for legislation, carving out private sovereignties in cyberspace, and even launching their own diplomatic missions. It's as if they looked at the state-dominated world order and thought, You know what? We can do better.

This transformation isn't happening in a vacuum. The rise of non-state actors coincides with a period of significant distrust in traditional institutions. People are looking for alternatives, and non-state actors with their flexibility and lack of bureaucratic baggage are stepping up to the plate. It's a bit like watching an underdog team come from behind; you can't help but root for them, even if it disrupts the established order.

But it's not all sunshine and rainbows. The increasing power of non-state actors raises questions about accountability. After all, who elected them? Who do they answer to, and how can they be reined in if their actions contravene public interest? It's a bit like inviting a genie out of its bottle — great in theory but messy in practice.

Furthermore, this shift toward non-state diplomacy introduces a complexity that traditional frameworks struggle to accommodate. It's challenging enough to negotiate between sovereign nations, but when you throw in a mix of MNCs, NGOs, and other groups, each with its own interests and agendas, you've got a recipe for diplomatic indigestion.

Still, for all their flaws and the challenges they pose, non-state actors are injecting a much-needed dose of dynamism into the staid world of diplomacy. They're forcing states to adapt, innovate, and reconsider the way they engage with the rest of the world. In essence, non-state actors are to diplomacy what punk rock was to music: a loud, brash reminder that there are always alternatives to the mainstream.

As we move forward, the line between state and non-state actors will likely become even more blurred. Hybrid entities that wield both economic power and political influence could emerge, further complicating the diplomatic landscape. It's an exciting, if uncertain, future — one that demands a reevaluation of our preconceptions about power and how it's wielded on the world stage.

In a nutshell, the role of non-state actors in modern diplomacy is a testament to the fluidity and complexity of international relations today. Like it or not, they're here to stay, reshaping the art and craft of diplomacy in ways that we're just beginning to understand. It's a brave new world out there, and the traditional actors in international relations might just find themselves playing catch-up.

So what's the takeaway for those of us watching from the sidelines? Perhaps it's that we should be prepared for a future where the power to influence global events doesn't solely reside with those who have a flag and a seat at the United Nations. In this new era of diplomacy, it's the non-state actors who might just hold the keys to the kingdom. And that, my friends, is a game-changer worth paying attention to.

Chapter 2:
The Tools of Influence and Manipulation

After dissecting the polished surface of modern diplomacy in Chapter 1, we now find ourselves peering into the toolbox that global powers quietly shuffle around in the shadows. As we all know, it's not just about who you know, but about what you can do that really twists the arm of the international stage. Enter the wide array of economic sanctions, that age-old tactic of giving a country the monetary silent treatment until they fall in line. But it doesn't stop there; we've moved past the era of simply cutting off trade. The digital age has ushered in the era of information warfare, where truth is malleable and reality can be tailored like a fine suit.

In this tango of influence and manipulation, the stakes are high, and the players are never quite what they seem. It's a world where economic levers are pulled with the finesse of a seasoned puppet master, creating ripples that can uplift or devastate economies with the flick of a policy pen. Then there's the shadowy realm of information warfare, where narratives are carefully crafted, and deploying a well-timed tweet can be as strategic as a military maneuver. Here, the battlefield is the global mind, and victory is measured in perceptions shaped and hearts won (or lost).

So as we navigate through these tools of modern diplomacy, keep in mind that behind every seemingly benign interaction on the world stage, there's a calculated game of chess being played. The pawns? Information and economic stability. The prize? Influence and power.

The Dark Side of Diplomacy

And in this game, understanding the rules doesn't just give you a seat at the table—it gives you the chance to change the game.

Economic Levers and Sanctions

So we've danced through the dark art of modern diplomacy and meandered through its evolution, from sneaky secret treaties to somewhat more transparent public agreements. Now let's shimmy down the rabbit hole into the world of economic levers and sanctions, shall we?

Imagine, if you will, a world where countries are like big old high school cliques. But instead of throwing shade or spilling tea, countries throw economic sanctions. That's right, when words fall short and military action is too hefty a card to play, in swoops the almighty power of economic pressure. It's less Mean Girls and more Game of Thrones, but with less blood and more boycotts.

Welcome to the not-so-subtle art of economic arm-twisting. It's like telling your neighbor, "Hey, if you don't stop playing the banjo at 3 a.m., I'm cutting off your Netflix access." But on a global scale and, sadly, without the banjo.

Now the thing with economic sanctions is that they're the go-to tool in the diplomatic toolkit. Don't like what another country is up to? Bam! Hit 'em with a sanction. Human rights violations? Bam! Sanction. Nuclear proliferation? Bam! You guessed it, sanction. It's the international relations equivalent of Oprah handing out cars, but less fun and more controversial.

But here's the kicker: While sanctions sound great on paper, their effectiveness is as debatable as pineapple on pizza. Sure, in some cases, sanctions have brought countries to the negotiating table. More often than not, they hurt the common folk. You know, the ones who can't influence nuclear policies or prevent their leaders from engaging in military conflicts in distant regions.

And then, there's the issue of economic levers as tools of influence. Think of it as financial incentives for good behavior, kind of like giving a dog a treat for not eating your shoes. "Here, good country, have some trade benefits and investment opportunities." It's carrot and stick diplomacy, but sometimes it feels like all we've got are sticks, and nobody's seen a carrot for decades.

It's time to talk about the big players: the United States and the European Union. When they wield the economic sanctions hammer, the ripples are felt worldwide. Companies scramble, stock markets twitch, and suddenly, everyone's checking whether their bank accounts are frozen. It's a global game of whack-a-mole, but with serious economic consequences.

However, it's worth noting that sanctioned countries frequently become skilled at evading measures. They find back doors, side doors, and sometimes even dig tunnels to circumnavigate sanctions. It's like watching a high-stakes episode of MacGyver, but nobody's laughing.

And in the twist of all twists, sometimes sanctions backfire. They can rally nationalistic fervor, making leaders stronger domestically, even as they're pariahs on the world stage. It turns out, nothing unites people like a common enemy, especially if that enemy is denying you your favorite imported cheese.

But wait, there's more! Sanctions can lead to strange bedfellows. Countries pushed into a corner by sanctions turn to others in similar situations or to those not particularly bothered by their actions. This can lead to new alliances, shifting the global balance of power in unexpected ways. It's the diplomatic equivalent of "The enemy of my enemy is my friend," with a side of "Let's trade in currencies that bypass the US dollar."

Of course, there's always a debate about morality. Imposing economic sanctions is like playing God with the global economy. It raises questions. Is it right? Is it effective? Is it just? Or is it merely a way to look tough on the international stage while avoiding real action? It's the geopolitical equivalent of posting a strongly worded tweet and thinking you've solved global warming.

Don't misunderstand: Economic sanctions and levers are important tools. They're part of the complex tapestry of international relations. But like any tool, they require wisdom, restraint, and, above all, a clear vision of the endgame. Without these, they're just blunt instruments that can cause more harm than good.

In a world that's increasingly interconnected, the ripple effects of sanctions are felt far and wide, touching everything from the price of gas to the availability of your favorite international snack. It's a reminder that in the global village, no country is an island, even if they're literally an island.

So as we navigate the murky waters of economic sanctions and levers, let's remember that with great power comes great responsibility. Or at the very least, an understanding that every action has a reaction, often in places and ways we can't predict. It's not just about flexing on the international stage; it's about understanding the complex, intertwined world we all share.

In the final analysis, economic sanctions and levers are not just tools of statecraft; they're testaments to the fragile, intricate web of global relations. They remind us that in the endless quest for influence and power, the line between persuasion and coercion is perilously thin. As we wield these tools, we can't forget the ultimate goal: a more peaceful, just, and cooperative world. It's a lofty goal, sure, but hey, aim for the stars, and you might just hit the moon. Or at least not crash the global economy in the process.

The Power of Information Warfare

We're entering the high-stakes domain of information warfare, where knowledge isn't simply power—it's a weapon. Amid the sophisticated arsenal of global influence, this tool stands out for its ability to operate in the shadows, often shaping perceptions and decisions without a trace.

At its core, information warfare is about controlling the narrative. It's a chess game on a global scale, with nations maneuvering to cast themselves in the best light—or their adversaries in the worst. The game's pieces? News articles, social media posts, hacked emails, and deepfakes. The players? Anyone from state-sponsored hackers to government agencies, and sometimes, groups or individuals with their own agendas.

The clever twist in this drama is the rise of digital platforms, turning what used to be a slow-burning conflict into a wildfire. In the blink of an eye, a well-crafted tweet can go viral, shaping public opinion in ways that were unimaginable even a decade ago. The speed and reach of information today have amplified the power of influence operations to an extent that is both awe-inspiring and terrifying.

There's no need to beat around the bush; some nations have turned this into an art form. They've mastered the craft of sewing discord, manipulating narratives, and even influencing elections in other countries. It's like watching a magician at work if that magician's tricks could shift the balance of global power.

One of the most insidious aspects of information warfare is its ability to blur the lines between truth and falsehood. In this arena, facts are malleable. Today's technology has given rise to sophisticated disinformation campaigns, where fake news is designed to mimic credible sources, making it increasingly difficult to discern fact from fiction.

The Dark Side of Diplomacy

The implications of this are profound. When public trust is eroded, societies become fragmented, more polarized. People start questioning the very foundation of their beliefs and institutions. From there, it's just a small step to undermining democracy itself. After all, how can you make informed decisions if you can't even agree on what's true?

It's not all doom and gloom, though. Just as information can be weaponized, it can also be a shield. Various initiatives aim to educate the public on media literacy, helping people navigate this complex landscape and recognize manipulation when they see it. It's akin to training a jedi to resist the dark side—equally nerdy, but far more relevant to our daily lives.

On the global stage, the battle lines in information warfare are not always drawn between nations. Non-state actors, including terrorist organizations and advocacy groups, have also entered the fray. They leverage social platforms to spread their messages, recruit followers, or even crowdfund their operations. It's a wild world where everyone has access to the megaphone, for better or worse.

In response, nations are ramping up their defenses. From establishing dedicated cyber command units to enacting legislation aimed at protecting against foreign influence, the countermeasures are as varied as they are critical. It's a digital arms race, with cybersecurity and information integrity at its heart.

Yet, for all its sophistication, information warfare is not without its risks for the perpetrators. Engaging in these tactics can backfire spectacularly. Just as misinformation can spread like wildfire, so too can the revelation of a state's involvement in such activities tarnish its reputation, inviting scrutiny and retaliation. It's a double-edged sword, wielded on a tightrope.

Consider for a moment the moral implications of this form of warfare. Traditional wars have rules, lines that aren't supposed to be crossed. But in the realm of information, those lines are muddier. Is it right to manipulate public opinion, even if it's in the interest of national security? Where do we draw the line between influence and indoctrination?

This brings us to the power dynamics inherent in information warfare. It's not just about who can shout the loudest, but also who can silence voices. Internet shutdowns, censorship, and the suppression of dissenting opinions are all tools in the arsenal of those looking to maintain control. Here, information warfare intersects with human rights, reminding us that the stakes extend far beyond the digital realm.

Looking ahead, the evolution of information warfare promises to keep us on our toes. Deepfake technology, artificial intelligence, and machine learning are set to take the manipulation of reality to unprecedented levels. Imagine a world where seeing is no longer believing, where every piece of information must be scrutinized for authenticity. It's both an exciting and a daunting prospect.

In conclusion, the power of information warfare lies not just in its ability to shape perceptions but in its potential to reshape the very fabric of society. As we navigate this Brave New World, our challenge is to harness this power for good, fostering an informed citizenry and defending the pillars of democracy. It's a tall order, but hey, nobody said being a global citizen was going to be easy. Let's just hope we're up to the task.

So as we pivot from the shadows of manipulation and control, we're reminded of the immense responsibility that comes with wielding information. In the end, it's about more than just influence—it's about integrity, transparency, and the pursuit of truth. Armed with these values, we stand a fighting chance in the ongoing battle for hearts and minds. The quest continues...

Chapter 3:
Economic Hit Man and Sovereign Subjugation

Welcome to an era where the global chess game isn't confined to traditional battlefields but thrives in boardrooms and stock exchanges, as revealed by the best-selling book Confessions of an Economic Hit Man. In this chapter, we're peeling back the curtain on the not-so-mysterious but certainly insidious world of economic hitmen. These are the smooth operators, cutting deals that would make a loan shark blush, all under the guise of development and aid. They're the masterminds behind the scenes, making sure that when a country is down, they're never truly out—as long as they're out in a way that benefits the global power players. We're talking about nations getting caught in the snare of debt so deep that the idea of sovereignty becomes more of a cute concept than a reality.

Imagine being at a fancy dinner where you're served a dish that you didn't order, can't afford, and, frankly, looks inedible. Yet, the waiter insists it's good for you, and by the way, you'll be paying for it for the next fifty years. That's a glimpse into how economic hitmen operate: serving up loans and aid packages with strings attached that would leave Gulliver tied down. Development, in their hands, becomes less about uplifting economies and more about laying the groundwork for strategic geopolitical advantage. We'll dive deep into a case study that's as enlightening as it is infuriating, showcasing how these practices aren't anomalies—they're the playbook.

So let's navigate the murky waters of international finance, where the politics of loans and bailouts reveal a battlefield that's both complex and compelling. This chapter isn't just a story of exploitation; it's an exploration of resilience in the face of sovereign subjugation. It's time to understand how countries are fighting back, renegotiating, and in some cases, breaking free from the clutches of economic subjugation. Buckle—oh wait, no metaphors about securing oneself—let's just say, prepare for a journey into the heart of modern economic warfare and the quest for financial independence.

Debt

We're going to explore a topic that's hotter than a summer sidewalk in Death Valley: debt. But not just any debt. We're talking about the kind that strangles nations, turning them into puppets controlled by the invisible hands of wealthier states and corporate giants. It's the Shakespearean tragedy of our modern political and economic sphere, only with less iambic pentameter and more spreadsheets.

So how does this whole debacle start? Imagine a nation, let's call it Country X, brimming with potential yet stifled by a lack of infrastructure or financial instability. Along comes a smooth-talking economic hitman from the Global North, promising the world or, at least, a dam, a highway, or a new financial center. The deal is sweet, or so it seems. Fast-forward a few years, and Country X finds itself in an economic chokehold, gasping for fiscal air.

The arithmetic of debt subjugation is brutally simple. Country X receives a loan that's ostensibly aimed at stimulating its economy or improving its infrastructure. However, the fine print ties Country X into a repayment scheme that's as forgiving as a loan shark three days after the due date. And just like that, the debtor is at the mercy of the creditor.

The Dark Side of Diplomacy

This isn't just a matter of dollars and cents; it's a dance of power and control. The indebted nation finds its policies and priorities dictated from afar. Need to slash social services to funnel money into debt repayment? Done. Open up pristine environments to mining operations by foreign corporations? Sure thing. The sovereignty of the indebted nation erodes faster than a sandcastle at high tide.

But wait, there's more. The interest rates on these loans are often the financial equivalent of high-speed highway robbery. Even as countries scramble to pay them off, the combination of high interest rates and economic policies imposed by the lenders ensure that the debt grows like a teenager during a growth spurt. It's a trap that would make Admiral Ackbar facepalm in despair.

Now you might think, surely there's a way out of this mess? Debt forgiveness, perhaps? Ah, but here's the rub. Debt forgiveness often comes with strings attached, strings that pull the indebted country even deeper into the sphere of influence of their creditors. It's akin to being 'rescued' by someone who then insists you live in their basement and do their chores ad infinitum.

The nefarious beauty of this system is its self-perpetuating nature. As countries become ensnared in debt, they lose leverage, making them susceptible to further exploitation. This could involve relinquishing control over essential resources, from minerals to ports, or even the rights to their own stories, as narratives are crafted by those holding the purse strings.

The morality play of this scenario unfolds on a global stage, but the villains aren't twirling mustaches or cackling at their own evilness. They're attending board meetings and signing off on memos, draped in the cloak of respectability and flanked by armies of lawyers. The weaponization of debt is done with a pen, not a sword, and its effects are insidiously profound.

Interestingly, the playbook for debt diplomacy hasn't changed much over the decades. From the banana republics, manipulated by fruit companies with the complicity of foreign governments, to the modern-day financial maneuvers that tether countries to fiscal time bombs, the script is eerily similar. Only the actors and the technology have evolved.

So what's the grand conclusion? Are we destined to watch as country after country falls prey to the debt trap? Not necessarily. The beauty of history is that it's full of unexpected twists. Just as nations have been pinned under the thumb of financial overlords, so too can they rise, mobilize, and rewrite the narrative. But it demands vigilance, solidarity, and a keen eye for the ever-changing tactics of economic hitmen.

Debt isn't just a set of numbers on a balance sheet. It's a weapon—one that can subjugate and control nations without firing a single shot. The irony is palpable; in a world that praises the virtues of freedom and sovereignty, the chains of debt bind tighter than any iron shackle.

As we proceed, let's not view the indebted nations merely as victims, but as battlegrounds where the fight for autonomy against economic imperialism is ongoing. The struggle is real, folks. It's about reclaiming the right to decide one's own destiny, free from the shadow of debt.

The dance of debt and power is a complex tango, requiring both awareness and action to change the tune. It's a story that unfolds daily, touching billions of lives, shaping economies, and defining the contours of global power. The next chapter in this saga depends as much on our collective action as it does on the maneuvers of the economic hitmen and their masters.

Remember, the world doesn't have to run on the terms set by a few. It's high time we rethink, resist, and redraw the lines. After all, the future is not set in stone, and paths to freedom are carved by those daring enough to challenge the status quo. Let's be part of that brave number.

Development

Now we embark on a journey into the murky waters of development to uncover how it's been molded into a tool for economic subjugation. Picture this: a country is struggling, its infrastructure crumbling, and along comes a seemingly benevolent figure offering a hefty loan for "development." Ah, the plot thickens, right? Because let's face it, when it comes to global politics, nothing is as straightforward as it seems.

Initially, these loans sound like a godsend, a quick fix to all the nation's problems. But here's the catch: the terms are often so predatory they'd make a loan shark blush. We're talking high interest rates, strings attached, and clauses that favor the lender, not the recipient. It's a classic case of economic imperialism, modern style.

The idea behind these loans isn't just financial gain; it's about control. By burying a country in debt, powerful nations can dictate its policies, its alliances, and, crucially, its resources. Ah yes, we're back to the age-old motivator: resources. Because beneath every "development" project, there's often a scramble for minerals, oil, or strategic access points.

It's important to bear in mind the role of the so-called development projects themselves. Infrastructures like dams, roads, and bridges are pitched under the guise of progress. Yet they often serve the interests of the lender, opening up markets and resources for exploitation. It's a bit like setting up a lemonade stand in someone else's yard and charging them for the pleasure.

And here's where it gets juicy: the contractors and corporations involved in these projects are frequently from the lender country. So not only are you lending money with one hand, but you're also scooping profits back with the other. It's a win-win—if you're the lender, that is. The borrowing nation, meanwhile, gets saddled with debt and projects that don't always meet their needs.

This model of development is pervasive, and its effects are devastating. Nations find themselves locked in a cycle of dependency, unable to break free from the financial shackles. It's a neocolonial chess game, and the pawns are real countries with real populations who suffer the consequences.

One disturbing trend is the commodification of water through these development projects. Imagine privatizing something as essential as water in countries struggling with access to it. It's like saying, "Oh, you were thirsty? Well, now you'll have to pay for every drop." It highlights a stark picture of where priorities lie in these so-called development agendas.

The irony of it all is that the very institutions claiming to fight poverty are often perpetuating it. By enforcing structural adjustments, these financial juggernauts ensure that borrowing nations are more focused on repaying debts than investing in their own people. Education, healthcare, and social services take a backseat to debt repayment—a cycle as vicious as it is intentional.

As for accountability, it's practically a foreign concept in these transactions. Corruption flourishes in the shadows of these massive projects, with kickbacks and bribes ensuring that only a select few benefit. It's a global heist, with the spoils divided among those in power while the majority are left with crumbs.

But here's the twist in the tale: resistance is growing. From grassroots movements to national policies aimed at rejecting these predatory loans, countries are beginning to fight back. It's a David versus Goliath battle, sure, but history has shown that Goliaths can fall.

Take Argentina's bold stance on restructuring its debt or Ecuador's audit that revealed the illegitimacy of much of its external debt. These are not just isolated incidents; they're part of a broader pushback against economic subjugation. It's a testament to the resilience and ingenuity of nations determined to reclaim their sovereignty.

Development should be about empowering nations, not enslaving them. It should be a collaborative process that respects the needs and visions of the people it aims to help. Anything less is exploitation, dressed up in the guise of aid.

As we navigate these complex issues, it's crucial to question the narratives we've been sold about development and progress. It's time to dismantle the systems that perpetuate inequality and envision a model of development that is truly inclusive and equitable. After all, the prosperity of the powerful should not be built on the subjugation of the weak.

In this global village of ours, the fates of nations are intricately linked. A model of development that upholds dignity, respects sovereignty, and fosters genuine growth is not just beneficial; it's essential. Only then can we move toward a world that values every nation's right to carve its own path, free from the shadows of economic hitmen.

It's a tall order, no doubt. But the first step in dismantling an unjust system is exposing its flaws. And that's precisely what we aim to do. So let's roll up our sleeves and get to work, shall we? Because the world deserves better, and it's about time we demanded it.

Case Study: Dominance The Politics of Loans and Bailouts

Embarking on an investigation into something as dry as yesterday's toast yet as scandalous as prime-time drama: the politics behind loans and bailouts. Now you might be thinking, "Loans and bailouts? Where's the drama in that?" Oh, hold on to your hats because this is where global power plays shine in all their dubious glory.

Imagine you're at a high stakes poker game, but instead of chips, countries are betting with their economies. This isn't just about cash; it's about influence, control, and keeping certain players in a perennial state of 'owing one.' The big guns—international financial institutions and some of the wealthiest nations—hold the deck, while smaller countries are trying to play their best hand with what they've got.

First off, let's talk about loans. On the surface, they appear as benevolent aids to struggling countries, promising economic development and stability. However, the reality is often a Faustian bargain. These loans come with strings attached—conditions and policies that often lead to the erosion of sovereignty. It's like inviting someone to rescue you from quicksand, only to find they're slowly siphoning off your rights as they pull you out.

Then there are the bailouts, the financial world's version of "saving" an economy from collapsing. It sounds noble until you realize it often results in austerity measures that cut deeper into the social fabric than any economic crisis. The irony? The politicos pushing these bailouts pat themselves on the back for saving the day, while millions struggle under the weight of increased poverty and reduced public services.

But why do countries fall into this trap? It's the seductive promise of quick fixes and the pressure to conform to a global economic standard that doesn't always fit. It's like trying to play a game where the rules were not only written by someone else but are also constantly changing to their benefit.

Consider Greece during the 2008 financial crisis—an illustrative tale of bailouts gone wrong. Here was a country grappling with debt, only to be 'saved' by a Troika of lenders enforcing crippling austerity. The result? A devastating impact on the Greek public, where the cure seemed more debilitating than the disease.

The Dark Side of Diplomacy

And then there's the issue of debt accumulation. It's not just about borrowing money; it's about creating a cycle of dependency. This cycle limits a country's policy options and keeps it within the sphere of influence of major powers or financial institutions. It's akin to lending someone an umbrella, then constantly reminding them it might rain whenever they try to make a decision for themselves.

What's deeply unsettling is the opacity of these deals. Behind closed doors, terms are negotiated that can alter the fate of nations. Yet the public, the very people affected by these decisions, are often kept in the dark, fed with promises that this is all for their own good.

However, it's important not to characterize all lenders with the same sinister brush. In some instances, loans and bailouts have provided necessary breathing space for economies to recover and grow. The problem isn't the concept of lending or helping; it's the power dynamics and conditions often embedded within these financial rescues.

So what's the takeaway from all this? It's that in the realm of global finance, loans and bailouts are not just about economics; they're about control, influence, and sometimes, subjugation. Countries must navigate these treacherous waters carefully, balancing immediate financial relief with long-term sovereignty and the welfare of their people.

To change this dynamic, there needs to be a shift toward more equitable financial practices. Transparency, fairness, and genuine cooperation should be the pillars of international finance. This means creating mechanisms where loans and bailouts are structured to empower, not subjugate, recipient nations.

However, achieving this is like turning a tanker; it's slow and requires collective will. Until then, the tale of loans and bailouts remains a cautionary one, a reminder that in the glitzy world of international finance, all that glitters is not gold, and the most generous offers may come with the heaviest chains.

In conclusion, the politics of loans and bailouts is a saga filled with heroes and villains, winners and losers. It's a narrative that unveils the complexities of global power dynamics, where economics serves as both the sword and the shield. As we move forward, let's hope for a plot twist—one where fairness, transparency, and mutual respect dictate the terms of engagement, rather than dominance and dependency.

Next time you hear about a country receiving a massive loan or a bailout package, look beyond the headline numbers. There's always a story behind the story, a tale of power, politics, and, often, exploitation. Understanding this is key to demystifying the shadowy world of global finance and moving toward a future where all nations can play the game on a more level field.

Chapter 4:
Behind Closed Doors:
The Reality of Diplomatic Intrigue

So we've walked through the glittering halls of diplomacy, where everything seems polished and just so diplomatically courteous. But let's not kid ourselves; when the doors close, the gloves come off. This chapter peels back the velvet curtain to reveal a world where whispers carry more weight than a public declaration. Ever wonder why some international agreements seem to come out of nowhere, almost like magic? No, it's not because our leaders suddenly found common ground while sharing a cup of tea. It's the intricate web of diplomatic intrigue, where backroom deals, secret handshakes, and whispered promises in the shadows dictate the course of our world. Imagine, if you will, a game of chess but with nations instead of pieces, and you're not too far off. We're going to dive into the murky waters of covert influence, where the only rule is that there are no rules. The stakes? Well, they couldn't be higher—economic dominance, political power, even the fate of entire nations. So ready to uncover the secrets behind those closed doors? Let's just say, diplomacy isn't always as diplomatic as you'd think.

Case Studies of Notable Diplomatic Maneuvers

Let's immerse ourselves into the thrilling world of diplomatic sleight of hand, where nations play the game of thrones but with embassies instead of castles. Ever wondered how countries manage to pull rabbits out of hats in the international arena? Well, buckle in—uh, I mean, prepare yourselves for a rollercoaster through some of history's cheekiest diplomatic maneuvers.

To start off, we'll discuss the time when the US secretly opened a dialogue with China in the 1970s. Picture it: a global chessboard, the Cold War at its frostiest, and then, bam! Henry Kissinger, playing the role of a political Houdini, sneaks into Beijing to lay the groundwork for President Nixon's visit. This move not only stunningly reconfigured global alignments but also shows that sometimes, the best diplomacy happens away from the prying eyes of the public.

Moving forward, it's important to remember the Cuban Missile Crisis—a truly tense moment in history. Here, John F. Kennedy and Nikita Khrushchev teetered on the brink of nuclear disaster. However, through a blend of public bravado and covert negotiations, they struck a deal that averted catastrophe. The true extent of their agreement remained shrouded in secrecy; while Russia pledged to remove their missiles, President Kennedy also agreed to withdraw US missiles from Turkey—a remarkable feat of diplomacy. The takeaway? A well-timed whisper can have monumental consequences.

Fast forward to the late 1980s, and we've got Mikhail Gorbachev opening the gates to the West with his policies of glasnost and perestroika. While hardliners at home gnashed their teeth, Gorbachev's diplomatic outreach essentially helped end the Cold War without a shot fired in anger. That's the power of diplomacy: changing the game by changing the conversation.

Then there's the Iranian nuclear deal, or JCPOA, as the wonks like to call it. A prime example of how torturous and drawn-out negotiations can lead to an agreement that, at least for a time, caps nuclear ambitions and opens up channels of communication between longtime adversaries. Whatever one's stance on the deal, its intricate dance of carrot-and-stick diplomacy showcases the complexity of modern international relations.

The Dark Side of Diplomacy

But hey, not all maneuvers are about avoiding global annihilation. Some are about winning without fighting. Take the European Union's expansion eastward post-Cold War, softly pulling in nations with the promise of economic prosperity and political stability. It's like saying, "Join our club, we have cookies," and suddenly, you've reshaped the continent.

Speaking of economic tactics, let's tip our hats to the sanctions game. Love them or hate them, sanctions are a go-to move in diplomatic toolkits. They're like saying, "Play by the rules, or we're canceling your credit card." Notable is their use against Iran and North Korea, aiming to bring defiant states to the negotiating table or at least cramp their style.

And we shouldn't gloss over Russia's annexation of Crimea. A bold geopolitical maneuver followed by a masterclass in diplomatic jujitsu to dodge the worst of international repercussions—at least for a time. It's a case of action first, negotiate the consequences later, proving that foregone conclusions aren't always so.

Remember when Qatar was suddenly blockaded by its neighbors? Here's where diplomacy gets sporty—literally. Through investments in global sports, Qatar not only boosted its international profile but also developed a web of soft power that helped it navigate a tight geopolitical spot. It turns out, owning half the world's sports teams isn't just for bragging rights.

Wrapping up our world tour, let's swing by Africa, where China's "Belt and Road Initiative" is changing the face of international relations one infrastructure project at a time. It's diplomacy with Chinese characteristics: build a port, win a friend. And though it's raised eyebrows around the world, it's undeniably reshaping global dynamics.

In the end, what do these tales of diplomatic intrigue teach us? That behind every handshake photo op, there's a saga of covert meetings, backchannel communications, and high-stakes negotiations. It's a world where silence can speak louder than words, and sometimes, the most impactful actions are those taken away from the limelight.

So the next time you see world leaders grinning for the cameras or making grand statements from podiums, remember: the real story is likely happening behind closed doors, in the quiet, shadowy recesses of power. And every so often, those stories slip out, giving us a fleeting glimpse of the art and craft of modern diplomacy.

As we've journeyed through these case studies, remember, diplomacy isn't just about avoiding war—it's about crafting a narrative, controlling the global conversation, and sometimes, rewriting the rulebook entirely. The world stage is a complex web of interests and intentions, where the clever, the brave, and sometimes the downright audacious make history in the shadows.

In closing, while these maneuvers can reshape the world, they also reflect the imperfections and moral ambiguities of international relations. In the grand chessboard of global diplomacy, pieces are moved in both light and darkness, guided by the dual hands of strategy and necessity. It's a reminder that in the pursuit of national interests, the line between right and wrong often blurs, leaving us to ponder the true cost of power.

Strategies of Covert Influence

With a martini, stirred, we will embark on a journey into the netherworld of diplomacy, where the shine of formal receptions dims in the shadow of covert operations awaits. It's a realm where influencing strategies unfold like a spy novel, except these tales are etched in the annals of realpolitik rather than fiction. Wrap your mind around the concept of power plays that aren't just about showing strength but manipulating perceptions, decisions, and, ultimately, history itself.

The Dark Side of Diplomacy

First up, we've got the age-old tactic of espionage. It's not all James Bond shenanigans with martinis and car chases. In the quiet rooms where the world's fate hangs by a thread, intel is king. You'd be stunned to learn how much of diplomacy is about who has the juicier dossier. The goal? To outwit and outmaneuver counterparts by knowing their intentions before they've even solidified them themselves.

Then there's blackmail, the darker twin of diplomacy. It's not just for soap operas. Imagine having leverage so powerful over another country's delegate that you can sway policies in your favor. Sounds like a plot twist, right? But it's a card often played behind the gilded doors of embassies and consulates.

Don't forget about the subtle art of disinformation. It's like painting a Picasso with lies—crafting a narrative so convincingly that even the target starts doubting what's real and what's not. Manipulating the media, planting stories, these are the tools that shape the public perception, turning the tide of diplomatic favor without firing a single shot.

Economic warfare takes it to another level. It's not just about sanctions, though those play a part. It's about making and breaking fortunes, about controlling resources so tightly that countries are forced into decisions they wouldn't otherwise make. Think of it as playing chess but with national economies.

Cyber operations have opened a new frontier for covert influence. Hacking isn't just for stealing secrets anymore. It's about manipulation on a massive scale: influencing elections, creating discord, even controlling the infrastructure of entire nations without setting foot on their soil.

Cultural diplomacy, on its face, seems benign, even beneficial. Yet beneath the veneer of promoting national heritage and fostering mutual understanding, there's a strategy at work. Influencing another nation's cultural scene can subtly shift public opinion in favor of the influencer, making it a soft but potent tool of covert influence.

Using non-state actors as proxies to achieve diplomatic goals is a strategy as old as statecraft itself. By supporting rebel groups, mercenaries, or even NGOs, states can advance their interests while keeping their hands ostensibly clean. It's a murky business, offering both plausible deniability and significant influence, if one knows how to play the game right.

Then there's the manipulation of international law. Twisting legal norms and exploiting loopholes can delay actions, tie up decisions in bureaucratic red tape, and frustrate the efforts of the international community. It's a game of who knows the rules better and, more importantly, who knows how to bend them without breaking.

The creation of alliances and pacts under the table is another prime strategy. These aren't your granddad's treaties, openly debated and signed with pomp. We're talking about informal agreements, promises made in the dark, that shape military, economic, and political landscapes quietly but profoundly.

Psychological operations, or psyops, take the battle for influence straight into the minds of the target. It's about more than just propaganda; it's about demoralizing opponents, breeding discontent among their populace, and sowing seeds of doubt that grow into full-blown crises.

Even humanitarian aid isn't beyond being used as a tool of covert influence. By positioning aid strategically, a state can gain access to key regions, sway public opinion, and even manipulate the policies of the recipient nation. It turns benevolence into a lever of power.

Proxy diplomacy is a fascinating twist, where third countries or entities are used to convey messages, offers, or threats that can't be directly communicated. It's like playing telephone across the global playground, except what's whispered at the end can change the course of international relations.

Lastly, there's the leveraging of diaspora communities. By engaging with the diaspora, states can exert influence indirectly, fostering relationships that can be mobilized for demonstrations, lobbying, and even espionage. It's a reminder that the reach of covert influence isn't bounded by borders.

Each of these strategies, employed with precision, can alter the global landscape without a single bullet fired or a treaty signed. It's the shadow dance of diplomacy, where moves are made in the dark, far from the public eye, yet the consequences unfold in the full light of day. Uncovering these strategies isn't just about peeking behind the diplomatic curtain; it's about understanding that in the world of international relations, what you see is rarely all there is.

Chapter 5:
The Ethics of Diplomacy: Justifiable Pressure or Exploitation?

So we've navigated through the murky waters of modern diplomacy and uncovered the tools nations wield to sway the tides in their favor. But now let's pivot and tackle a beast of a different color: the ethical quagmire that this world of diplomacy often finds itself sinking into. You might be asking, where does one draw the line between applying healthy pressure and outright exploitation? That's the million-dollar question, or perhaps in the language of international negotiations, the billion-dollar bailout question. It's a fine line, my friends, finer than the hairline of a seasoned diplomat trying to sell you the idea that economic sanctions are just friendly nudges for compliance. This chapter is not just a journey; it's a tightrope walk over the Grand Canyon of moral ambiguity, where we'll scrutinize whether the ends really do justify the means or if we're all just playing a rigged game where the house always wins. From arm-twisting nations into unfavorable treaties under the guise of peace, to strategic alliances that look more like high school cliques, it's all under the microscope. Brace yourself for an exploration that's less about finding definitive answers and more about asking the right questions. Questions that might just make you see international diplomacy through a less-than-rose-tinted lens.

The Line Between Persuasion and Coercion

So here we are, diving headfirst into the murky waters of diplomacy's ethics. The line between persuasion and coercion? It's thinner than your favorite politician's promise. Imagine you're at a party. Persuasion is offering someone a drink to enjoy the evening. Coercion, on the other hand, is making them feel like they won't be invited next time if they don't accept that drink. Funny, right? Except, when nations play this game, the stakes are slightly higher than a social faux-pas.

In the arena of international relations, persuasion is the golden child. It's dinner invitations, handshakes, and lavish compliments. But when those handshakes become a bit too firm, bordering on a wrestling grip, we've entered coercion territory. This is where economic sanctions, military threats, and political isolation come into play. They're kind of like telling someone, "Nice economy you got there. Would be a shame if something happened to it."

But where do we draw this elusive line? It's like trying to find the edge of a circle. The truth is, the line is constantly shifting, muddied by power dynamics, historical contexts, and the eye of the beholder. One country's "gentle nudging" might be another's "aggressive shove out the door."

Take economic sanctions, for example. They are the go-to tool for asserting pressure. Yet they often affect the common populace more than the elites, pushing the boundaries of ethical action. Is starving an already struggling population really a justified means to an end? It's the equivalent of cutting off the electricity because your neighbor won't turn down their music. Sure, it might work, but at what cost?

Then there's the power of persuasion through media and propaganda. It's like being the most popular kid in school and using your influence to spread rumors. Before you know it, everyone's wearing the same brand of sneakers not because they want to but because they're afraid of not fitting in. That's information warfare for you—subtle, effective, and ethically dubious.

It's critical not to overlook military intervention, the ultimate form of coercion. It is like showing up to a knife fight with a bazooka. Sure, you might "win," but everyone's going to be a bit wary of inviting you anywhere after that. Military presence is often justified with terms like "peacekeeping," but there's nothing peaceful about tanks rolling through your backyard.

The argument often made for coercion is that it's for the greater good. That's like saying, "I'm hacking your social media for your own safety." Comforting, right? The road to hell is paved with good intentions, and international politics is no exception. The problem arises when the line between "for your own good" and "for our own good" gets blurred.

So how do we navigate this ethical minefield? It's a bit like finding a clean spot on a toddler's face—theoretically possible, but practically a challenge. Diplomacy, at its core, should be about mutual respect and understanding. It's recognizing that other nations have their own will, interests, and right to make decisions. Not just treating them like chess pieces on a global board.

In the cutthroat realm of international relations, the ideal often takes a backseat to the practical. The trick is to not let the car crash in the process. Persuasion should be about influencing decisions through positive means, not arm-twisting. It's about presenting a choice, not an ultimatum. That's the art—and the challenge—of true diplomacy.

Yet coercion happens. And when it does, it's crucial to ask: Who benefits? It's like looking behind the curtain in a magic show. More often than not, the answer reveals a lot about the intentions behind the actions. And here's the kicker: If the primary beneficiary is the coercing party, chances are we've veered off the path of ethical diplomacy.

Finally, walking the line between persuasion and coercion in diplomacy is akin to tightrope walking in a hurricane. It's precarious, fraught with moral dilemmas, and there's a hefty price to pay if you lose your balance. Yet it's essential for maintaining international harmony and respect. So the next time you hear about a country applying "pressure" or "influencing" another, take a moment to ponder: Are we talking about a friendly persuasion or a coercive arm twist? Because in the grand scheme of things, how we choose to engage with one another on the world stage defines not just the present moment, but the legacy we leave for future generations.

In the end, the difference between persuasion and coercion, much like beauty, lies in the eye of the beholder. But remember, when the line gets too blurred, it might just be time to put on a new pair of glasses. Or, in the case of international diplomacy, perhaps a new perspective on ethical engagement. Because at its heart, diplomacy should strive to bring us together, not tear us apart. And in a world that's already as divided as a high school cafeteria, that's something worth aiming for.

Now as we step back and look at the big picture, it's clear: The distinction between persuasion and coercion is not just academic. It's about the soul of diplomacy itself. In navigating these tumultuous waters, the choices we make today will echo in the halls of history. Let's make sure they're not echoes of regret.

International Responses and Regulations

It's quite the tightrope walk, this business of ethics in diplomacy. We've sauntered past the velvet curtains and caught a glimpse of the gritty backstage, where the magic of diplomacy reveals itself as equal parts persuasion and, let's be real, coercion. But in this murky realm, how are the globe's bigwigs reacting, and what rules of the game are they trying to enforce to keep things from going off the rails? Buckle up—metaphorically speaking—and let's dive in.

First off, international responses to the ethical quandaries of diplomacy are as varied as the countries that engage in them. It's a bit like trying to get cats to march in a parade—theoretically possible, but good luck. Some nations champion the cause of transparency and mutual respect, while others view diplomacy as a no-holds-barred arena where ends justify means. The result? An international patchwork of regulations that aims to set boundaries while allowing room for maneuvering.

In this zigzagging landscape, the United Nations (UN) emerges as the self-appointed referee, attempting to uphold international law and mediate disputes. But the UN's influence often feels like that of a hall monitor amidst schoolyard bullies. It proposes frameworks and agreements—think the Vienna Convention on Diplomatic Relations—but enforcing these norms is another story. Sovereign nations nod in agreement, fingers crossed behind their backs.

Then there's the World Trade Organization (WTO), spinning its own web of rules to ensure that economic pressures—frequently used as diplomatic leverage—play within certain lines. The idea is noble: level the playing field so that the economic Goliaths can't just trample Davids underfoot. Yet in practice, it's a delicate dance of power plays, with developed countries often setting the tune.

Regional organizations like the European Union (EU) and the African Union (AU) throw their hats into the ring too, crafting codes of conduct for their member states. Their efforts underscore the belief that closer neighbors might just adhere to a shared rulebook, reducing backyard brawls. The EU, for instance, wields the power of sanctions and incentives among its members, pushing for a collective front on issues like human rights and fair governance.

Nevertheless, it's important not to gloss over the elephant in the room: the mighty United States and its approach to wielding power on the world stage. With a foreign policy toolkit that includes everything

The Dark Side of Diplomacy

from economic sanctions to, shall we say, "persuasive" diplomacy, the US frequently sets trends in how international regulations are respected—or sidestepped. Sometimes it feels like watching a high-stakes poker game where the US holds a lot of the chips.

China, on the other hand, prefers a strategy of economic entanglement, weaving its Belt and Road Initiative like a spider web that ensnares other nations in indebted diplomacy. It's a long game, one that raises eyebrows and stirs debates on sovereignty and undue influence. The international community watches, sometimes aghast and other times in admiration, at the sheer scale of China's ambitions.

Now amidst all these players and their diverging strategies, there's a growing call for a digital Geneva Convention. The cyber realm, after all, is the new frontier of diplomatic skirmish, where battles are waged in the shadows, and the rules are still written in pencil. Countries like Russia, with their alleged meddling in elections, and North Korea, with its penchant for cyber heists, underline the urgent need for global norms in cyber conduct.

Yet, for all these grand plans and international declarations, the truth is that diplomacy often boils down to who has the bigger stick, or rather, who can swing it without getting caught. Sanctions, for instance, are a favorite stick wielded with abandon, intended to discipline rogue states but often crippling the common folk instead. It's a blunt instrument in what should be a surgeon's toolkit.

And what about espionage, the shadowy underbelly of international relations? Every nation denies it, every nation indulges in it. It's the open secret of the diplomatic world, a game played with a wink and a nod. Here, regulations tread lightly, if they dare to tread at all. After all, who polices the police?

The reality is, despite the plethora of international responses and regulations, a considerable gray area remains. It's a realm where morals are malleable and the ends often justify the means. It's diplomacy at its most raw, stripped of the niceties and handshakes that grace the public stage.

Yet there's hope. Amidst the diplomatic free-for-all, a new generation of policymakers is emerging. They advocate for diplomacy that doesn't just pay lip service to ethics but embeds it in action. They push for transparent agreements, accountable practices, and genuine respect for sovereignty and human rights.

As we stand at this crossroads, the future of diplomacy hangs in the balance. The path forward is fraught with challenges and temptations to revert to old, shadowy practices. But the call for a more ethical approach is growing louder, championed by those unwilling to accept that might makes right.

Overall, the quest for justifiable pressure without crossing into exploitation is a tightrope act that tests the mettle of nations. It's a constant battle between idealism and realism, between what should be done and what is done. But amidst this struggle, there lies a chance—a chance to redefine the ethics of diplomacy for a world that desperately needs it.

As we navigate this complex landscape, let's keep in mind that the power of diplomacy lies not just in the strength of our economies or militaries but in the integrity of our actions. After all, in the grand theater of international relations, the most enduring legacies are those built on a foundation of respect and mutual understanding. May the future of diplomacy be shaped by those brave enough to envision a world where power is measured not by how much pressure we can exert but by how wisely we wield it.

Chapter 6:
The Shadows Over Resource Wars

As the curtain rises on the theater of resource wars, you'd think it's all about drilling and mining, straightforward and on the surface. But oh, how the plot thickens once you peek behind the scenes! It's like watching a satirical play where the actors forget their moral compasses backstage. The battle for energy and minerals isn't just a scuffle over who gets the last bite of the pie; it's a full-blown saga with twists and turns that would make your head spin. Weaker nations, rich in resources but poor in power, find themselves caught in the crossfire of a narrative they hardly get a line in. It's a shadowy duel where the weapons are economic levers, covert operations, and, let's not forget, the ever-so-charming façade of diplomatic engagement.

Imagine the globe as a chessboard, but some players have got their hands on the board and are tilting it to let the pieces slide their way. The hidden battle for energy and minerals isn't just about securing resources; it's about asserting dominance, pushing boundaries, and sometimes, making sure the 'little guys' stay in their place. Amidst this, the plight of weaker nations is akin to a tragic monologue amidst a play of giants—heard but hardly acknowledged. This chapter isn't just a recount of who did what in the dark; it's a spotlight on the covert strategies and the silent screams of nations caught in the game they never wished to play. Strap in as we dive deep into the shadows over resource wars, where the narrative is twisted, the stakes are sky-high, and the moral of the story is often lost in translation.

The Hidden Battle for Energy and Minerals

So we've turned the page on diplomatic decorum and civility, and now we're digging into the messy, grimy details of what's really powering our global tug-of-war. Pull up a chair, and let's chat about the world's insatiable appetite for energy and minerals, shall we? It's a tale as old as time but with a modern, high-stakes twist.

In the corridors of power, the hunt for resources isn't just a subplot; it's the main event. You've got countries throwing elbows, using everything in their arsenal to secure access to the lifeblood of the 21st century: oil, gas, rare earth elements, you name it. It's less about keeping the lights on and more about keeping the upper hand in global geopolitics.

Securing a sustainable future or advocating for green energy isn't the primary focus of the energy battle, and portraying it as such would be misleading. It's a gladiator match overseen by nations and corporations, betting big on controlling the planet's veins of essential resources. Sure, they'll talk a good game about renewable energy, but watch where they send their mining equipment and military advisors. Actions speak louder than press releases.

Consider, for a moment, the Arctic. Once a pristine expanse of ice, it's now the latest battleground in the resource wars. As the ice melts, revealing untapped reserves of oil and gas, countries are scrambling to lay claim. It's like watching a group of kids discover a hidden stash of candy—except these kids have nuclear weapons and advanced drilling technology.

Or how about Africa? The continent is a treasure trove of minerals critical for modern electronics. Cobalt, coltan, you name it. The catch? These resources are often found in places plagued by conflict, corruption, and exploitation. Enter the scene: foreign miners with deep pockets and dubious ethics, making deals that would make a mobster blush.

The Dark Side of Diplomacy

Then there's the South China Sea—waters more crowded than a New York subway at rush hour, thanks to overlapping claims on oil and gas reserves. Naval standoffs and shadowy operations are the order of the day, as countries jostle for position. It's less Pirates of the Caribbean and more Game of Thrones with drones and submarines.

On the flip side, there are unforgettable rare earth elements—those obscure metals that sound like something from the periodic table's B-list but are actually A-list stars in the tech world. They're crucial for everything from smartphones to missile systems. Guess who has a near-monopoly on them? Yep, China. And guess who's not thrilled about that? Everyone else.

The result? A mad dash to find alternative sources, including under the sea. That's right, we're now eyeing the ocean floor, ready to disrupt ecosystems in our quest for technological dominance. It's like the gold rush, but underwater and with less respect for environmental regulations.

Amidst all this, you'd think there'd be a concerted effort to dial back our dependency on these resources, right? Well, not exactly. The transition to renewable energy is happening, but it's a slow burn, pun intended. In the meantime, the battle for conventional resources rages on, fueled by a paradoxical mix of denial, greed, and short-term strategizing.

And don't be fooled—this isn't just a game for nation-states. Multinational corporations are in on the action, too, wielding influence and lobbying governments to secure their interests. Sometimes, they're the puppet masters, pulling the strings behind the scenes, shaping policy, and bending the rules of international engagement.

What's the solution, then? If there were an easy answer, we'd have found it by now. What's clear is that solving the puzzle requires thinking beyond the next fiscal quarter or election cycle. It demands a reimagining of our global energy strategy, one that prioritizes sustainability and equity over geopolitical muscle-flexing.

It's a tall order, sure. But the alternative—continuing this hidden battle ad nauseam—isn't exactly appealing. The costs are too high, both environmentally and ethically. Plus, it's a game where even the winners end up losers in the long run, stuck in a cycle of dependency and conflict.

So as we close this chapter, let's keep one thing in mind: The real battle isn't over who controls the world's energy and minerals. It's over who controls the future. And in that fight, the weapons of choice won't be drills and submarines, but innovation, cooperation, and foresight.

Yes, the road ahead is fraught with challenges, and the stakes couldn't be higher. But if history teaches us anything, it's that when push comes to shove, humanity has a knack for pulling off the inconceivable. Here's hoping we channel that spirit once again, for the sake of our planet and future generations. Because when you strip away the geopolitical posturing and corporate maneuvering, that's what's really at stake here.

And with that, we turn the page, leaving the shadows of resource wars behind, hopeful for a future where energy and minerals aren't sources of conflict but pillars of a more sustainable, peaceful world. It's a lofty goal, but hey, aiming high never hurt anyone. Onward to brighter, less contentious chapters!

The Plight of Weaker Nations

Unveiling a global stage rarely illuminated—the weaker nations, those countries sitting on the edge of your news feed, overshadowed by the glitz and glamour of power politics—provides a different perspective. It's a narrative thick with the scent of exploitation, whispered deals, and the relentless pursuit of resources. In the world's relentless hunger for energy and minerals, these nations often find themselves caught in a web not of their own weaving.

Imagine a game of chess, but the pieces move themselves, fueled by a mix of desperation and coercion. That's the ongoing saga of resource wars, where the kings and queens are global powers and multinational corporations and the pawns are the weaker nations, rich in resources but poor in the means to defend their autonomy. It's a classic tale of might over right, where the rules are written by those who can wield the most influence.

In this lopsided game, economic levers and sanctions become weapons of choice. It's a world where "economic assistance" often comes with strings attached, strings that might as well be chains. These chains bind the hands of local leaders, compelling them to make deals that favor the wealthy nations while their own people see little of the profits.

The power of information warfare cannot be understated here. The narrative surrounding these weaker nations is carefully crafted by those who stand to gain the most. Stories of corruption and instability are magnified, painting these nations as too fragile to manage their wealth, creating a self-fulfilling prophecy that justifies foreign intervention.

Yet, amidst this seemingly grim reality, these nations are not merely victims. Resistance simmers beneath the surface. There are leaders and citizens alike who push back against the tide, trying to reclaim their sovereignty. Their battles are uphill, fought in the shadows of diplomacy and within the corridors of international forums.

International responses and regulations, designed to protect these nations, often fall short. It's a sobering reminder that in the world of global politics, ideals often buckle under the weight of economic interests. The line between persuasion and coercion blurs, and what passes for international diplomacy can sometimes resemble a high-stakes poker game.

The hidden battle for energy and minerals unfolds in stark contrast to the public face of international cooperation. Behind the veneer of diplomatic niceties lies a scramble for control over resources that can make or break economies. In this scramble, weaker nations are often seen not as partners but as territories to be exploited.

Within this context, the role of non-state actors becomes crucial. From multinational corporations that straddle the globe with their vast networks of influence to NGOs that navigate the choppy waters of international aid, these entities play a pivotal role in shaping the destinies of these resource-rich yet economically fragile nations.

As the world moves toward a new multipolar reality, regional tensions and shifting alliances further complicate the plight of these nations. The emerging power dynamics disrupt old relationships, making it even more challenging for weaker nations to find their footing and assert their interests on the international stage.

The impact of global governance—or occasionally, the lack thereof—on these nations cannot be overstated. In a system where might often equals right, the governance structures that are supposed to ensure fairness and equity instead often mirror the inequalities and injustices they aim to eradicate.

Proxy wars, another chapter in the saga of international interference, cast long shadows over these nations. These conflicts, while ostensibly about ideology or territorial disputes, often boil down to control over resources. The soils of these nations become battlegrounds for proxy wars, with little regard for the human cost.

This narrative isn't just about exploitation and coercion; it's also a testament to resilience and resistance. Across these nations, there are stories of grassroots movements, local leaders, and everyday citizens standing up to protect their rights, their resources, and their sovereignty. It's a reminder that while the battle may be uphill, it is not unwinnable.

The international community stands at a crossroads, facing a choice between continuing down the path of exploitation or forging a new, more equitable path that respects the sovereignty of weaker nations and recognizes their right to manage their resources. The time is ripe for a shift in how global powers approach resource-rich, economically weaker nations.

Amidst the global chess game of resource wars, it's easy to lose sight of the human element, the communities whose lives are irrevocably changed by the battle for resources beneath their feet. It is their stories that remind us of the stakes involved, lending urgency to the call for change.

In conclusion, the plight of weaker nations in the shadows over resource wars is a complex tapestry of exploitation, resistance, and the ongoing struggle for sovereignty. It's a narrative that demands not just our attention but our action. As the global community looks toward the future, the choices made today will shape the world of tomorrow, for better or for worse.

Chapter 7: Regional Tensions and the New Multipolar World

We're now venturing into a domain as capricious as a journey in a hot air balloon, holding a drink, with no knowledge of where we'll touch down. In this arena, the term 'tug-of-war' doesn't quite cut it when we talk about the global stage. We've moved past the times when a single heavyweight could dominate the ring. Instead, welcome to the bustling, jostling multipolar world where regional tensions simmer like a pot on the brink of boiling over. The globe has turned into a chessboard where major players are not solely countries anymore but bloated egos with every move closely scrutinized for a hint of weakness. These power shifts are about as subtle as a neon sign in a monastery, with alliances morphing faster than a quick-change artist. It's a space where wielding influence is a fine art practiced in the dark corners of international politics and where the impact on global governance is about as gentle as a sledgehammer. Remember, in this multipolar chaos, the rulebook is constantly being rewritten by those who can't afford to lose, driven by the pressing need not just to participate, but to dominate, manipulate, and, if necessary, flip the table over to ensure the game is never fair.

Shifting Alliances and Power Balances

Time to explore the nitty-gritty of the jaw-dropping ballet called geopolitics, where countries pirouette and occasionally step on each other's toes in the scramble for power. It's like watching that high-drama soap opera where alliances are as stable as a house of cards in a windstorm. We're at a juncture where old friendships are getting moldy, and new alliances are popping up like mushrooms after rain.

Consider the pivot to Asia, where the US is trying to court countries with the finesse of a lovestruck teenager, aiming to build a bulwark against China's irresistible rise. Meanwhile, China with its Belt and Road Initiative is cozying up to anyone with a port and resources, wrapping countries in a hug that's a tad too tight for comfort.

Then there's Russia, doing its best impression of a swashbuckling rogue, trying to resurrect its past glory. It's throwing weight around its neighborhood, rekindling old friendships and starting new romances with countries disillusioned by the West. The way Russia and China are giving each other googly eyes, you'd think they're plotting a romcom, not a strategic partnership.

Don't even get me started on the Middle East—a region that redefines the meaning of complicated. It's a web of alliances that would make your head spin faster than a dreidel on Hanukkah. Here, enemy-of-my-enemy logic is taken to heart, resulting in a kaleidoscope of shifting partnerships that can give you whiplash.

In Africa, things are equally dynamic. Everyone wants a piece of the resource pie, and countries are playing it smart, flirting with multiple suitors. They're not just passive objects of affection in geopolitics' love triangle; they're leveraging their options like a pro at speed dating.

Europe's landscape is no picnic either. The EU is struggling to maintain unity while navigating the treacherous waters of nationalism and populism. Brexit was like a messy breakup that made everyone bitter and anxious about the future of this continental relationship.

Then you have the technology factor, throwing in a curveball into traditional geopolitics. Cyber capabilities are the new nuclear weapons, and everyone's trying to get the slickest hackers on their side. It's like watching a cyberpunk thriller where virtual alliances are as crucial as physical ones.

Trade wars are also reshaping alliances. Countries are using tariffs like passive-aggressive notes in a roommate situation, causing friction and forcing others to pick sides. It's a global game of "Who's my BFF?" but with billion-dollar stakes.

Climate change, believe it or not, is another player in this geopolitical soap opera. Countries are banding together to combat this existential threat, forming green alliances that sometimes cross traditional geopolitical lines. It's like Mother Nature decided to crash the party and force everyone to get along.

Amid all this, non-state actors are having a field day. Corporations, NGOs, and even individuals are wielding power that can rival states. They're influencing policies, brokering deals, and sometimes throwing a wrench in the works just for the fun of it.

So in this whirlwind of changing dynamics, who's winning? It's hard to say. The US is trying to cling to its superpower status with the desperation of a reality TV star past their prime. China is the ambitious newcomer, ready to do whatever it takes to take the lead. Russia is the wildcard, unpredictable and nostalgic for a past glory.

But here's the kicker: In a multipolar world, power isn't about having the biggest army or the fattest wallet. It's about being the most adaptable, the most persuasive, and sometimes, the most underhanded. It's about forming alliances not just for the sake of power but for survival.

As we watch this drama unfold, it's essential to remember that behind every strategic move, there are people's lives at stake. The decisions made in air-conditioned rooms and behind closed doors can determine the fate of millions.

So what's next in this high-stakes game of geopolitical chess? Will we see a world where alliances are based on shared values and mutual respect, or will it be a free-for-all, where might makes right? One thing's for sure: The game is on, and it's more complex than ever.

In the end, understanding the shifting alliances and power balances is key to navigating this new multipolar world. It's not just about knowing who's up and who's down; it's about understanding the motivations behind the moves and predicting what comes next. Because in the end, the goal isn't just to survive; it's to thrive in a world that's constantly changing.

The Impact on Global Governance

In today's world, the impact on global governance is colossal. We're living in an era where the geopolitical chessboard is less about black and white squares and more about a Jackson Pollock Painting—messy, colorful, and open to interpretation. In the realm of global governance, the emergence of a multipolar world has thrown traditional rules out the window and initiated a free-for-all match where every player is vying for influence, and only the strongest will survive.

The concept of a unipolar or even a bipolar world seems like a quaint relic of the past. Now we have major players emerging from every corner of the globe, each with their own ambitions and tools of influence. This newfound diversity in global power dynamics has turned international forums into battlegrounds where alignments are fluid and agreements are as stable as a house of cards in a tornado.

Take, for instance, international organizations like the United Nations. Once seen as the pinnacle of global governance, these institutions are now often criticized as being too slow to respond, bogged down by bureaucracy and prone to being hijacked by the interests of powerful member states. It's like trying to perform a synchronized swimming routine in a pool with sharks.

The rise of regional powers has only added to the complexity. These entities are no longer content with being secondary actors and have started to assert their interests more aggressively. It's like a high school drama where previously overlooked characters are now demanding main roles, disrupting the conventional storylines.

This multipolar world has also seen an uptick in soft power and hybrid warfare. Countries are now engaging in a multifaceted game of chess, utilizing economic levers, cyber capabilities, and cultural influence to sway outcomes in their favor. It's less about who has the biggest army and more about who can control the narrative and manipulate the economic threads that bind countries together.

Furthermore, the shifting alliances and power balances have introduced an era of unpredictability in global governance. Agreements and treaties are now subject to the whims of national leaders, whose decisions can be influenced by anything from economic pressures to a particularly persuasive tweet. It's a world where traditional diplomacy dances to the tune of social media tempests and populist waves.

Amid this chaos, smaller states find themselves navigating a labyrinth of challenges. With the giants playing their games, these countries must align themselves smartly to protect their interests without getting squashed. It's akin to playing hopscotch on a minefield—trepidatious and precarious but unavoidable.

The environmental arena, too, has felt the impact of these shifting dynamics. Climate change negotiations are a clear example of how global governance is strained by differing national interests with progress often hampered by those who view environmental regulations as anathema to economic growth. It's like trying to convince arsonists that fire is bad—they just don't see it or choose not to.

The rise of non-state actors further muddies the waters of global governance. Multinational corporations, NGOs, and even terrorist organizations wield influence that can rival, or at least significantly challenge, that of sovereign states. It's as if there are shadow puppeteers pulling strings behind the scenes, shaping outcomes according to their clandestine agendas.

On a similar note, the digital realm has emerged as a new frontier in the struggle for power. Cyber diplomacy and information warfare have become central components of international relations, with states engaging in digital skirmishes that can have real-world consequences. In some cases, a hacker with a laptop has more sway than a diplomat with a treaty.

This new multipolar world also raises questions about the nature of sovereignty and non-interference, principles that have long underpinned international law. In an age where influence operations, cyber attacks, and economic coercion can deeply affect the internal affairs of states, these concepts are increasingly under strain. It's like watching magicians argue about which tricks are fair game—while the audience's pockets are being picked.

The implications for global governance are profound. The international community must adapt to this new reality, crafting mechanisms that can accommodate the diverse interests of a multipolar world while still promoting collective action on shared challenges. Not an easy task by any means—it's like trying to herd cats, if the cats were armed with nuclear weapons.

In practical terms, this might mean reforming existing international institutions to give a greater voice to emerging powers, developing new forums that can address the specific concerns of different regions, and innovating diplomacy to manage the complexities of modern statecraft. Essentially, it's about building a bigger, more inclusive table—while ensuring it doesn't collapse under its own weight.

Yet amidst all the chaos and complexity, there lies an opportunity. This new multipolar world has the potential to foster a more equitable and diverse international order, one where different perspectives are heard and respected. It's an opportunity to move away from a system dominated by a few powers to one that reflects the rich tapestry of global humanity.

So as we wade through the tumultuous waters of contemporary global governance, let's not despair at the challenges. Instead, let's embrace them as opportunities to build a more nuanced, inclusive, and effective system of international relations. Because at the end of the day, it's not just about managing power—it's about harnessing it for the greater good. If that sounds like a tall order, well, it is. But what's life without a few challenges to keep things interesting?

Chapter 8:
Proxy Wars and Their Global Impact

So here we are, diving headfirst into the murky waters of proxy wars and the ripples they send across our big blue marble. At first glance, proxy wars seem like a chess game, but don't be fooled; this is chess with live ammunition, where the pawns bleed and the kings rarely face the music. These conflicts, often seen as the go-to strategy for nations itching to flex their muscles without getting their hands dirty, have become the hallmark of modern geopolitical strategy. They're the kind of wars where big powers pick a side, often in someone else's backyard, load them up with arms, and then cheer from the safety of their own borders. Whether it's the Cold War classics in Latin America and Southeast Asia or the more recent scorched earth dramas unfolding in Ukraine and Syria, proxy wars are the unsolicited gifts that keep on giving tragedy and instability.

But why bother, you might ask? Well, it's all about influence and control, with a generous side of economic interests, garnished with a sprig of ideological zeal. These conflicts allow major players to tilt the global balance of power, pouring gasoline on local conflicts for global gains. It's like playing the stock market but with human lives, national sovereignty, and the principles of international law. And not to mention how they're a breeding ground for violations of human rights and humanitarian laws. The worst part? The aftermath. When the dust settles, the local populations are left holding the bag, trying to rebuild from the ruins while the instigators of their misery casually pivot to the next strategic interest, leaving a legacy of chaos, resentment, and unexploded ordnance.

Understanding the proxy wars in Ukraine and the Middle East, as well as Africa's complex battlegrounds, isn't just about unpacking tales of sorrow and strife. It's about connecting the dots to see the bigger picture of international politics where global stability is often sacrificed at the altar of strategic advantage. These conflicts are not isolated incidents; they're interwoven into the fabric of global relations, influencing everything from refugee flows to international trade policies. As we peel back the layers, it becomes evident that the impact of proxy wars stretches far beyond their immediate battlefields, shaping the world in ways both seen and unseen, often to the detriment of peace and prosperity. So while the puppet masters continue their game, it's crucial for the rest of us to recognize these maneuvers for what they are and work toward unwinding this tangled web of covert conflicts. After all, in the end, the game of proxy wars is one where there are no real winners, just varying degrees of loss and a world left picking up the pieces.

Understanding the Proxy Wars in Ukraine and the Middle East

Now easing into the murky waters of modern warfare, where battles aren't always fought between the armies of warring nations but often outsourced to third parties. Yes, we're talking about proxy wars, a favorite pastime of global powerhouses who'd rather not get their hands dirty—or, let's be real, caught. The stage for such conflicts? Lately, Ukraine and the Middle East have been popular choices.

Starting with Eastern Europe, the crisis in Ukraine isn't just a local skirmish over land or identity. It's a chess match between the West and Russia, with local forces and volunteers moving the pieces. It's a proxy war, all right, where NATO's invisible hand meets the Kremlin's shadow, both pushing their agendas under the guise of support and solidarity. Because, of course, openly throwing troops into the mix would be too 20th century.

Now, flip the globe to the Middle East. The area is a tapestry of conflicts, each more complex than the last. Syria, for instance, is the ultimate proxy war playground, with the US, Russia, Iran, and Turkey all having a slice of the pie but using local factions and militias to do the baking. It's a buffet of foreign interests, seasoned with ideological and sectarian spice. Deliciously disastrous.

We can't forget about the ever-combustible playground of Yemen, a place where Saudi Arabia and Iran play tug-of-war with human lives. This proxy conflict has turned the country into a humanitarian disaster, proving that in the game of thrones, the pawns suffer the most.

But why, oh why, do powerful nations love the proxy war strategy? First off, it's the secrecy and deniability. "Who, me? No, we didn't send those troops. Must've been someone else." It's politics and warfare with a mask on, enabling countries to push their agendas without the international backlash of direct involvement.

Then there's the cost—much like outsourcing customer service, proxy wars are economically more viable. Why spend your own resources when you can support a local group to do your bidding? Plus, it keeps the war "over there," protecting the instigator nation's soil from becoming a battleground.

Another delightful aspect (if you're into dark, geopolitical irony) is how proxy wars allow for testing of new military tech and strategies. It's like a live-action battle royale, where superpowers can see how their latest drones or cyber warfare tactics fare in real conditions, with real lives at stake. Morbid? Absolutely. True? Unfortunately.

But it's not entirely bleak. Sometimes, believe it or not, proxy wars can lead to unexpected alliances and diplomacies. The enemy of my enemy is my friend, right? This age-old adage becomes especially relevant, creating fleeting partnerships between countries that would otherwise be at each other's throats.

Of course, the human cost of these geopolitical games is devastating. Proxy wars displace millions, destroy infrastructures, and set nations back decades in development. The scars left on the land and people in Ukraine and the Middle East are a testament to the proxy war's lasting damage.

Yet the merry-go-round of proxy warfare spins on, with global powers continually adjusting their strategies. It's a dance of domination and influence, where nations vie for the upper hand without stepping onto the dance floor. Stealthy, cunning, and utterly devastating in its impact.

One must ponder, in the long run, who truly benefits from such conflicts. The arms dealers, the political elites, the shadowy advisors whispering in the ears of power? It's certainly not the common folk, who are caught in the crossfire of ambitions and ideologies they might not even subscribe to.

The ripple effects of proxy wars extend far beyond the immediate combat zone. They foster a culture of mistrust and paranoia, complicate international diplomacy, and sometimes backfire spectacularly (think supporting a group that later turns against you).

So what's the endgame? Can the cycle of proxy wars ever be broken, or are we doomed to watch history repeat itself with new players but the same old strategies? It's a question worth pondering as we reflect on the global impact of these hidden wars.

Overall, the proxy wars in Ukraine and the Middle East serve as stark reminders of the complexity and tragedy of modern conflict. They underline the necessity of seeking innovative solutions to international disputes and the urgency of addressing the underlying issues fueling these fires. Maybe, just maybe, we can find a path to a more peaceful and just world order. But then again, in the world of international politics, hope often seems like a strategy designed for the optimists and dreamers.

So there you have it. A whirlwind tour of the proxy wars tearing through Ukraine and the Middle East. It's a messy, intricate web of conflict that defies easy solutions. But understanding is the first step toward action, and awareness is the key to change. Or so we hope, in our ever-optimistic pursuit of a world where proxy wars are studied in history books, not the morning news.

Africa's Struggle within the International Chessboard

Imagine the African continent as this gargantuan chessboard, where instead of knights and pawns, you have countries and militias being moved around by invisible hands. Sounds like the plot of a bad spy novel, doesn't it? Well, it's the harsh reality. The players in this game? The usual suspects—former colonial powers, the United States, China, Russia, and a handful of others, each with their own agenda, ready to topple governments or prop up regimes as long as it suits their interests.

Why Africa? It's not just about the vast natural resources or strategic ports. It's also the voting bloc in international bodies like the United Nations that makes Africa an attractive arena for global powers. And a front to the fight against terrorism or, more cynically, the convenient excuse it provides for military intervention.

The narrative isn't new. During the Cold War era, Africa was the stage for proxy wars with the Soviet Union and the West backing opposing sides in Angola, Mozambique, and Ethiopia, to name a few. Fast forward to the 21st century, and not much has changed, except the players have gotten more sophisticated, and the stakes have gotten higher.

Enter China—not with guns blazing, but with infrastructure projects and investments. The Middle Kingdom's approach could be seen as neo-colonial, gunning for influence through economic means. It's like playing chess with cash instead of strategy. And let's not kid ourselves; it's not altruism driving these investments but a calculated move to secure resources and political influence. Yet, somehow, this soft power play is rewriting the rules of the game in Africa.

Not to be outdone, the United States and France, among others, have military bases dotted across the continent. Ostensibly there to combat terrorism and piracy, these bases also ensure that their influence in the region isn't waning in the face of China's economic onslaught. The guise of counterterrorism operations often masks the underlying strategic interests. It's almost as if there's an unspoken rule in international politics—never let a good crisis go to waste.

Russia, too, has entered the African theater, not with the ideological zeal of the Soviet Union but with a pragmatic approach to expand its influence. Through military contracts, arms deals, and security training, Russia positions itself as an ally for unstable regimes looking for support without the strings of democratization or human rights attached.

Then there's the role of African leaders themselves, playing into the hands of foreign interests for personal gain or political survival. Some exploit the competition among the superpowers, maneuvering for more aid, defense contracts, or diplomatic support to cling to power, often at the expense of their country's sovereignty and the well-being of their population.

The consequences for the African populace are dire—from civil wars and coups to humanitarian crises. These aren't just side effects; they're often direct outcomes of this cynical game of geopolitical chess. The proliferation of arms, support for militant groups, and political meddling destabilize regions for years, if not decades, leaving ordinary Africans to bear the brunt.

Amidst this struggle, there's a glimmer of resistance and agency from within the continent. African Union missions and regional initiatives show that African countries are not merely pawns to be moved around. They're capable of strategic moves themselves, whether it's peacekeeping operations or negotiating blocs in international forums.

However, we must not sugarcoat it—the road ahead is daunting. Breaking free from the strings of external powers while dealing with internal challenges requires a level of political will and unity that's been elusive. It's a bit like trying to play chess while others are playing checkers on the same board; the rules aren't the same, and the goals are often at odds.

What does this mean for the future? It's anybody's guess. But one thing's for sure: Africa's strategic importance isn't waning anytime soon. The continent could redefine the international order, shifting from being the chessboard to being one of the players—a transition that's not just possible but necessary.

Beyond the geopolitics, there's a human element that often gets lost. Behind every resource deal or military base are communities whose lives are upended. This isn't just a game—it's about the future of millions of people whose voices are seldom heard above the noise of international diplomacy.

As we unpack the dynamics of Africa's struggle within the international chessboard, let's not forget the resilience and agency of its people. Their narratives are key to understanding the continent's past and its potential to shape its future. The game is far from over, and Africa is not out of moves.

The events that have transpired since 2020-2023, with back-to-back anti-colonialist military coups rocked the Western African region, indicate that political dynamics are changing across the continent and that Africa as a whole is moving in a new direction.

In essence, Africa's story on the international stage is a complex web of ambition, manipulation, and resistance. As global dynamics shift, the continent has an opportunity to assert itself more forcefully, navigating the treacherous waters of international relations to carve out a more equitable and autonomous position. The struggle is real, but so is the potential for change. And while the game of chess might be slow and methodical, Africa is steadily making its moves, challenging the status quo and redefining its role on the international chessboard.

Chapter 9:
The Clandestine Operations to Gain Regional Dominance

Whisper it quietly, but not all battles for dominance involve tanks rolling across borders or diplomats furiously waving sanctions around. Nope, some of the juiciest bits of international intrigue happen in the shadows, where the spies play. In this chapter, we're diving into the murky waters of clandestine operations, those secret maneuvers countries perform to get one over on their neighbors without firing a single shot. Think of it as chess, but if the pieces could wiretap and sabotage each other while the rest of the world pretends not to notice. Using a blend of realpolitik and straight-up espionage, these operations range from election interference that'd make your grandma blush to funding opposition movements so discreetly that even the beneficiaries scratch their heads about where that last wad of cash came from. It's like watching a magician at work—except the magician's trick is destabilizing a government, and the rabbit pulled out of the hat is often a new regime that just happens to fancy the magician's home country a tad more. And while the ethics might be as murky as a teenager's Internet history, the long-term effects on global politics are undeniable. Countries emerge as regional powerhouses not just by their economic muscle or military might but by how well they can pull strings from the shadows. So pull back the curtain and take a peek at the art of gaining regional dominance through the kind of operations that definitely won't make it into the history books, but absolutely should.

B. K. Chaaraoui

Case Studies on Covert Interventions

In the grand, shadowy theater of global politics, covert operations are the secret scripts from which the world's power plays are directed—though seldom acknowledged publicly. Behind the veil of official diplomacy, covert interventions shape the contours of regional dominance with the finesse of a sculptor—albeit one working in the dead of night. This exploration peels back the curtain on some of the most strategic, yet unspoken, maneuvers that have redrawn the map of influence.

Take, for example, the classic coup d'état—a staple in the covert operator's playbook. Often, the narrative is woven around promoting democracy, but scratch the surface and you'll find interests as varied as control over natural resources or countering geopolitical adversaries. Historical precedents abound; a whisper of "regime change" and suddenly, governments more pliable to foreign interests are miraculously in power, despite the often violent upheavals this causes locally.

Another tool of the trade is the fostering of insurgencies. Arms, training, and funds flowing in from our foreign "benefactors" tend to prop up one group against another, stoking fires that can burn out of control. The fine print of these operations often gets lost in translation, cloaked under the guise of supporting freedom fighters—until they're deemed terrorists when the geopolitical winds shift.

Economic warfare, too, plays a critical role. Sanctions, embargoes, and financial manipulation carry the invisible hand of coercion, forcing nations into corners from which the only escape is alignment with larger powers. It's a high-stakes game of poker where one's economy could be collateral damage, all in the name of exerting pressure without firing a single shot.

Information warfare cannot be overlooked. Crafting narratives, spreading disinformation, and exploiting the media have become weapons as effective as any armament. The goal? Shape perceptions, sow discord, and manipulate the outcome of elections, thereby installing leaders amicable to the orchestrators of these campaigns.

Indeed, the digital realm has opened new frontiers for covert operations. Cyber-espionage and cyber-sabotage can undermine nations' security, steal sensitive information, and even cripple infrastructure, all while the aggressor remains hidden behind layers of plausible deniability. It's like the old days of spy-vs-spy but with keyboards instead of cloak and daggers.

We must not overlook the involvement of non-state actors. Mercenaries, private corporations, and NGOs can play pivotal roles in covert operations, offering both deniability and expertise. Their involvement is a testament to the outsourcing of influence, a clear sign of how covert operations have evolved to suit the modern age.

In dissecting these operations, one can't help but marvel at the complexity and audacity of these endeavors. From propping up dictatorships to fomenting revolutions, the range is as broad as it is consequential. The aftermath, however, isn't always as rosy as the architects might hope. Unintended consequences can emerge, from prolonged conflicts to humanitarian crises, often leaving the affected regions worse off than before.

Consider the Middle East, where covert operations have both shaped and shattered nations. The legacy of such interventions has led to decades of strife as foreign powers, vying for control over the region's vast energy resources, have played kingmaker with little regard for the long-term stability of the region.

In Latin America, too, the Cold War era saw a flurry of covert activities aimed at containing political ideologies deemed unsuitable by the dominant powers. The resultant political upheaval and human rights abuses still echo across the continent.

Africa has not been spared, with its valuable minerals and strategic positioning making it a fertile ground for covert tug-of-wars. Here, proxy wars and the exploitation of ethnic tensions have left scars that are still healing, demonstrating how interventions can deeply fracture societies.

Asia's narrative intertwines with the tales of covert operations aimed at curtailing the spread of certain political philosophies, ensuring access to critical sea routes and maintaining the balance of power in a region that's pivotal to global economics. The complexity of these interventions often mirrors the intricate geopolitics of the area.

The justifications given for these covert interventions often center on maintaining national security, promoting democratic values, or ensuring the stability of the global order. Yet the question lingers: For whom are these benefits truly realized? It appears that more often than not, the real motivations are cloaked in the language of altruism, while the underlying rationale is far more self-serving.

Peering into the shadows, one finds a world where morality is ambiguous and the end justifies the means. Yet this Machiavellian approach to foreign policy, while potentially delivering short-term gains, often sows the seeds of long-term instability and resentment. It's a high-wire act, with the safety net of international law and human rights hanging loosely below.

Overall, the covert interventions discussed serve as a stark reminder of the complexity and murkiness of international relations. While they might be executed in pursuit of regional dominance, their repercussions often ripple outwards, affecting global governance and the very fabric of international peace and security. As the world becomes increasingly interconnected, the ramifications of these shadowy operations—intended and unintended—reverberate more widely, challenging us to reconsider the paths to influence and power in the 21st century.

Covert Ops Chronicle

In the dark corridors of global politics, shadows were being cast over the crowns that adorned the grand stage; and out of this emerged a trilogy of missions that would come to shape nations and change history. These stories read like high-octane tales of ambition, betrayal, and intrigue, complete with their very own rosters of villains, opportunists, and dupes.

A range of existing intrigues and tales kicked off with the sensational 'Operation Ajax' in Iran in the mid-20th century:

Operation Ajax (1953, Iran)

Amid the Cold War paranoia of 1953, Iran faced growing unrest. Mohammad Mosaddegh, the resolute nationalist premier, might not have been popular enough to satisfy our simplistic patriotic desires. Instead, he suffered domestic betrayal from unexpected enemies, sparing him further martyrdom and ending the era of desperate political martyrdom tactics. By then prime minister, his nationalization of the Anglo-Iranian Oil Company enraged Britain and its new friend, the United States. The whole international conspiracy was created by these four countries under the name Operation Ajax, led by CIA agent Kermit Roosevelt Jr.

This chaos overtook Tehran, brought on by bribery, street protests, and propaganda, weakened Mosaddegh's leadership. Eventually on August 19, 1953, a second coup was staged, and Mohammad Reza Pahlavi returned from exile and reclaimed the throne. What happened in the years after, unfortunately, was a slide into authoritarianism and deep-seated anti-Americanism that eventually congealed into a revolution in 1979.

Operation PBSUCCESS 1954, Guatemala

In the jungles of Central America, a year later, the United States once again planned and carried out a secret overthrow. The United Fruit Company, a great American corporate Goliath, viewed the land reforms of Jacobo Árbenz, the progressive president of Guatemala, as a menace. The CIA was apprehensive of a shift left in Guatemalan policies under Árbenz. This they acquired in the person of military officer Carlos Castillo Armas, a man with dreams of his own. Supported by propaganda, misinformation, and strategic bombings, Armas and a US-trained rebel force overthrew the Árbenz government, establishing a pro-US regime.

The takeover inflicted Guatemala with decades of violence, oppression, systematic human rights violations, and civil war. It set the stage for US intervention in Latin America during the Cold War.

The Congo Crisis (1960)

It shone for a while in Central Africa, this light on the horizon, before being extinguished by the scheming of the Cold War. Patrice Lumumba, Congo's first democratically elected prime minister, had set out to claim the Congo's independence, a path to their sovereignty, their justice. But his nationalist beliefs and income of independence also put him against Western forces —the US and Belgium specifically —that had been concerned over the potential of a Russian-operated Congo.

The CIA was similarly aided by the deepest ambition of a military leader, Joseph Mobutu, masquerading as patriotism under the direction of Lawrence Devlin. With the help of finance, they conducted a psychological operation and created a division in the government of Lumumba, which resulted in his arrest, transfer to the secessionist forces, and the killing that took place on January 17, 1961. Mobutu seized power with US support, giving rise to a ruthless dictatorship which would mark the Congo for decades to come.

Operation Condor and South America in the 1970s

United States-backed coups and dictatorships shook Latin America politically in the 1970s. President João Goulart succumbed to rightwing and US fears about a leftist tide that pulled the rug out from under his moderate reforms in Brazil. The CIA-backed coup had resulted in a military junta that crushed dissent, supported US interests, and dug scars that would last until a return to civilian rule in 1985.

The socialist reforms of President Salvador Allende in Chile were seen as a menace to the US hegemony. The CIA sowed the seeds of a bloody 1973 military coup by instigating covert operations and economic sabotage to foster the conditions for Pinochet to seize power. Then came the 1976 coup in Argentina, which unleashed the "Dirty War," and thousands disappeared. All of these with the exception of Maza were allies of Operation Condor, the clandestine network that tried or defanged leftist movements throughout the continent.

Operation Cyclone (1979-1989, Afghanistan)

The more rugged and mountainous Afghanistan was able to furnish the US with yet another theater for its ideological war against communism. When Soviet troops invaded to help their Marxist allies in Kabul, the US had other ideas. Billions of dollars went into Pakistan's intelligence agency, who then funneled money to arm the Mujahideen in one of the largest schemes of a covert operation ever run by the CIA: Operation Cyclone.

Using the latest US arms, the fighters put up a tough resistance that eventually pushed the Soviets into leaving. However, the result was a carnage as warlords fought for control of the country. The instability created conditions for later violent groups, such as al-Qaeda.

The Iran-Contra Affair, 1980s, Nicaragua

The Reagan administration conducted it by proxy, covertly backing the Contras, an insurgent group made up of right-wing paramilitaries, within Nicaragua. Even though Congress had prohibited US funding, the administration went to illicit arms sales to Iran and used the proceeds to fund their allies. The Iran-Contra scandal would become one of the most to-the-point political scandals of the period.

The Invasion Of Iraq (2003)

And then came Iraq. TEHRAN — The specter of the September 11 attacks hung heavily over American foreign policy at the time, and the Bush administration regarded Saddam Hussein of Iraq as a threat that had to be eliminated. Based on flimsy evidence that no other nation agreed upon, the US spearheaded a coalition to invade Iraq and quickly bring down the regime of Hussein.

But peace proved elusive. Insurgency, factional bloodshed, and crumbling state institutions soon made the occupation a quagmire. Into the vacuum came ISIS, a manifestation of satanic cruelty that left behind a black mark on the security of the world.

Timber Sycamore 2012–2017

Timber Sycamore was a classified weapons supply and training program carried out by the United States Central Intelligence Agency (CIA) and supported by some Arab intelligence services, including officials in Saudi intelligence. The program was intended to overthrow Syrian President Bashar al-Assad. Established in 2012 or 2013, it supported Syrian opposition militias fighting al-Assad in the Syrian civil war with money, weapons and training. The program, which was run by the CIA's Special Activities Division, has trained thousands of rebels, US officials said. CIA activities in Syria were most notable in 2013 when President Barack Obama said behind closed doors that he would increase the arming of the fighters similar to what we are seeing now in Ukraine. The one-time program was revealed to the public in mid-2016.

Legacy

Covering the gritty streets in Tehran, right through to the wild jungles in Guatemala, these undercover operations etched their mark into the walls of the world. They expose a dance of ideology, ambition, and fear, in which democracies were weakened and dictators were emboldened, a machination whose steps remained secret and the fates of nations were rewritten.

Long-Term Effects on Global Politics

Continuing from our discourse on the covert moves to clinch regional dominance, we uncover the profound and far-reaching implications these clandestine operations have on the intricate web of global politics. And, boy, do these waters run deep! It's like throwing a pebble into a pond, except the pebble is a covert operation, and the pond is the fragile ecosystem of international relations.

First up, trust—or should I say, the erosion thereof. When countries get caught with their hands in the cookie jar, it doesn't exactly inspire confidence among their peers. Trust, once the bedrock of diplomatic relations, begins to erode faster than a sandcastle at high tide. In essence, we're witnessing a global trust recession. Countries start double-guessing each other's motives, leading to a paralysis in international cooperation. Remember the kid who cried wolf? Well, imagine if half the playground was crying wolf, and you'll get the picture.

Then there's the weaponization of information. If knowledge is power, then misinformation is a power surge that shorts the entire system. The long-term effect? A political landscape where truth is more malleable than Play-Doh. It's a world where facts are contested and narratives are as stable as a house of cards in a wind tunnel. The consequence for global politics is straightforward—policies based on distorted realities, leading to solutions that solve nothing.

Not to gloss over the destabilization of regions. The aftermath of foreign intervention often leaves a void, and nature abhors a vacuum. This void is rarely filled with rainbows and unicorns. More often than not, it's chaos that takes the reins, as we have seen in Afghanistan, Iraq, Libya, Sudan, and Syria. This chaos doesn't recognize borders; it packs its bag and tours globally. The domino effect of regional instability can topple nations far beyond the initial intervention zone, making it a Pandora's box of global proportions.

Moving on to arms races and military escalations. When countries feel threatened, they don't sing "Kumbaya"; they stockpile weapons. This escalation can lead to a precarious balance, where peace is maintained not by mutual respect but by mutual assured destruction. Think of it as a very, very tense standoff between neighbors, except instead of garden hoses, they're brandishing nuclear missiles.

On a lighter note, it is worth considering the cultural impact. The global narrative begins to shift. Pop culture starts soaking up these themes of espionage, betrayal, and power plays, reframing the global political discourse as a spy thriller. Movies, books, and TV shows no longer just entertain but shape public perception of international relations. It's diplomacy by Netflix, and it's as bizarre as it sounds.

The rise of proxy conflicts is another side effect. As direct conflict becomes less palatable, powers engage in a shadow boxing match, using third parties to fight their battles. This not only exacerbates conflicts but also muddies the waters of accountability. It's a geopolitical "Whodunnit?" where everyone knows whodunnit, but no one can prove it.

The Dark Side of Diplomacy

Moreover, it is crucial that we consider the significant impact on global governance. The narrative of "us vs. them" stiffens, deepening divides and making international consensus as rare as a unicorn sighting. Multilateral institutions find themselves on shaky grounds, struggling to navigate a world where the rules of the game are constantly being rewritten—often in invisible ink.

Furthermore, the economic repercussions can't be ignored. Sanctions, trade wars, and economic espionage become tools in the arsenal of international diplomacy, leading to a balkanization of the world economy. We start to see a fracturing of global trade networks as countries retreat into economic silos, hedging against perceived threats.

Environmental policies also suffer. Global challenges like climate change require a unified response, yet the trust deficit and geopolitical rivalries foster a fragmented approach. It's akin to trying to solve a jigsaw puzzle when half the pieces are being hidden under the table.

We can't forget the human toll. Migration crises often follow the destabilization of regions as people flee from the chaos unleashed by these covert operations. The resultant strain on international relations and resources is immense as countries grapple with the influx of refugees seeking safety from a storm they had no hand in brewing.

The ripples even extend to technology, as cyber warfare and surveillance become part and parcel of international relations. The global quest for technological supremacy spills over into espionage, leading to an arms race in cyberspace. It's the Cold War 2.0, with the Internet as the battlefield.

In terms of global health, pandemics have shown that cooperation is key to tackling widespread crises. Yet in a world fragmented by distrust and competition, coordinated responses are hampered, leading to prolonged suffering and setbacks in global health advancements.

However, it's not all doom and gloom. These challenges also serve as a catalyst for change, driving innovation in diplomacy, international law, and governance structures. They prompt a reevaluation of the principles underpinning global politics, pushing for a more transparent, equitable international order. Or, at least, one can hope.

To wrap up, the clandestine operations to gain regional dominance are not just a skirmish in the shadows; they are battles that shape the terrain of global politics. Their long-term effects weave through the fabric of international relations, leaving a tapestry that is as intricate as it is volatile. As we move forward, understanding these subtleties is crucial in navigating the murky waters of global diplomacy. And who knows, maybe, just maybe, we'll learn to swim better together.

Chapter 10:
The Influence of Non-Governmental Organizations (NGOs) and Multinational Corporations (MNCs)

So after tumbling through the rabbit hole of global antics, we find ourselves at the intersection of two of the most prominent forces in today's diplomacy after we have traveled the intricacies of global issues. Non-governmental organizations and multinational corporations are two of the most important to grasp and analyze the powers to be reckoned with all the noise. NGOs, those self-proclaimed knights in shining armor, roam the global stage, swinging the sword of moral high ground, often dipping their toes—heck, their whole legs—into the murky waters of political influence. They start with a heartwarming tale of humanitarian aid, but don't be fooled; before you know it, they've wiggled onto the negotiation tables, whispering sweet nothings into the ears of those who pen the fate of nations.

On the flip side, MNCs strut across the world with their coffers full, leaving a scent of dollar bills in the air. Imagine this: a corporate giant waltzes into a developing nation, flashes a smile, and suddenly, it's shaping policies like it's molding Play-Doh. These behemoths, draped in the allure of economic progress, often dictate terms that would make sovereign states blush, all under the guise of "foreign investment." Look closely, and you'll notice the strings attached to their hefty contributions, steering foreign policies with the finesse of a puppeteer.

We shouldn't get lost in the illusion that one is the hero and the other the villain, though. This dance between NGOs and MNCs, twirling around the pillars of global governance, is a spectacle of modern influence. Their ballroom? The very stage of international politics where the boundaries blur between altruism and ambition, philanthropy and power. And as they tango, swaying the course of nations with each step, one can't help but wonder: In this grand performance of diplomacy, who really leads? Spoiler: it's a complicated relationship, but damn, it makes for an intriguing analysis. So don't just stand there on the sidelines; let's dive into the thick of it, shall we?

NGOs: From Humanitarian Aid to Political Influence

Once upon a time, in a world not so different from our own, nongovernmental organizations, or NGOs as we affectionately call them, started their journey as the good Samaritans of our global village. Armed with nothing but a deep desire to make the world a better place, these organizations plunged into the depths of humanitarian crises, offering a helping hand to those in desperate need. It's a tale as old as time, or at least as old as the concept of organized charity, but stick with me.

Fast forward to the present, and the NGO landscape has undergone what can only be described as a seismic shift. No longer are they seen merely as impartial messengers of goodwill and carriers of aid; they've morphed into political powerhouses, wielding influence that extends far beyond the field hospitals and refugee camps. How, you ask? Well, consider they've graduated from the school of hard knocks with a major in realpolitik.

The transformation didn't happen overnight. It was a gradual evolution, spurred by the realization that to genuinely impact the root causes of the crises they were fighting, they had to play the game. The game of politics, that is. And play it they did, stepping into the arena with a determination that would make even the most jaded of political strategists take notice.

NGOs began to harness the power of information, understanding that in the modern world, knowledge is not just power—it's superpower. They started crafting narratives, shining a spotlight on injustices that would otherwise remain in the shadows, and in doing so, they captured the attention of the public and policymakers alike. It's like they discovered the political equivalent of clickbait, only much less annoying and way more impactful.

But it wasn't just about making noise. NGOs started to play the long game, embedding themselves within the mechanisms that drive international policy. They became the advisors whispering in the ears of those in power, the experts called upon to testify in parliamentary hearings, and the negotiators sitting at the table during peace talks. Some might call it influence peddling; I call it strategic positioning.

Of course, with great power comes great scrutiny. Governments and multinational corporations, once the sole navigators of the international political seas, began to view NGOs as formidable adversaries. Allegations of bias and hidden agendas started to fly like confetti, painting these organizations as puppeteers maneuvering in the shadows. A tad dramatic, perhaps, but it underscores the shift in perception and the unease that comes with disrupted power dynamics.

The irony, though, is palpable. These very accusations often come from entities whose transparency records are as clear as mud on a rainy day. But that's a tale for another chapter. For NGOs, the criticism is a double-edged sword, challenging them to maintain their integrity and independence while engaging in the political fray.

We shouldn't gloss over the ethical tightrope NGOs must walk in this new era. The balance between advocating for change and maintaining neutrality is as delicate as it is crucial. Venturing too far into political activism can erode the trust of those they aim to help, yet steering clear of politics altogether is akin to bringing a knife to a gunfight in the battle against global issues.

In navigating these murky waters, some organizations have risen to prominence, becoming almost celebrity-like in their status. Their leaders are featured in glossy magazines, and their campaigns go viral, championed by influencers and the public. It's a strange world when hashtags have the power to mobilize international action, but here we are.

Yet this celebrity status is not without its drawbacks. The blurring lines between advocacy and sensationalism, between genuine activism and branding, pose significant challenges. The quest for funding, media attention, and public support can, at times, overshadow the very causes these organizations pledge to serve.

Despite these challenges, the political influence of NGOs cannot — and should not — be understated. They've become key players in the global arena, advocating for human rights, environmental protection, and social justice. Their ability to mobilize public opinion and effect change at the policy level has redefined the boundaries of what non-state actors can achieve.

But it's important not to get carried away. The ascent of NGOs into the political stratosphere is not a fairy tale with a guaranteed happy ending. It's a complex narrative, filled with triumphs and tribulations, strategic victories, and moral quandaries. It's a testament to their resilience and adaptability, but also a reminder of the perpetual tension between idealism and pragmatism.

As we look to the future, the role of NGOs is poised to become even more significant. As the lines between humanitarian aid and political activism continue to blur, these organizations will face new challenges and opportunities. The political landscape is ever-changing, but one thing remains clear: NGOs are no longer just on the sidelines of power—they're helping to shape it.

So what can we take away from this twisted tale of transformation? Perhaps it's the realization that in the quest to change the world, NGOs have themselves changed. They've outgrown the simplistic label of 'do-gooders' and emerged as strategic actors in their own right, capable of influencing the highest levels of power. It's a plot twist worthy of a blockbuster, and I, for one, can't wait to see what the next chapter holds.

In closing, we need to give credit where credit is due. NGOs have shown that with tenacity, creativity, and a willingness to engage in the messy art of politics, even the most deeply entrenched issues can be tackled head-on. It's a lesson for us all, really: never underestimate the power of determined individuals (or groups) to make a difference. And with that, let's turn the page and delve into the world of multinational corporations—but that's a story for another section.

MNCs and Their Role in Shaping Foreign Policy

Gone are the days when multinational corporations (MNCs) were mere economic entities; they've morphed into behemoths with enough clout to shape the foreign policies of sovereign nations. Now, how's that for a plot twist in the realm of global diplomacy? It is a fascinating concept to explore the labyrinth of influence and manipulation, where the lines between corporate interests and national security blur faster than a speeding bullet.

Imagine a world where the dollar sign is mightier than the sword. Sounds like a cliché, right? But in the era of globalization, MNCs have amassed so much power, they practically sit at the negotiation table, whispering sweet nothings into the ears of policymakers. The irony is, they don't even have to whisper; their presence alone speaks volumes. For starters, the economic footprint of some of these giants rivals the

GDP of entire countries. Now, if that's not leverage, I don't know what is.

When a company has the capacity to sway entire economies by either investing or divesting, you bet it can throw its weight around in the diplomatic arena. Employment, technology transfer, trade balances—these are no longer mere facets of econ textbooks; they're the bargaining chips in high-stakes geopolitical poker games. And guess who's holding the aces? Yep, the MNCs.

But wait, it gets juicier. Ever heard of 'economic diplomacy'? It's this neat trick where countries use their economic muscle to push their foreign agenda. Now add MNCs to the mix, and you've got yourself an explosive cocktail of influence peddling. These entities can open doors that diplomats only dream of knocking on. Need to soften up some sanctions? There's an MNC for that. Want to gain a foothold in a strategically important region? Call in the big guns, i.e., the giant corporations.

The symbiosis between MNCs and governments isn't exactly breaking news. But the audacity, the overt maneuvering—that's what's breathtaking. Take, for example, how energy companies lobby for or against foreign interventions, depending on what suits their interest. Or how tech giants can be arm-twisted into becoming inadvertent players in the global surveillance saga. It's not just about money; it's about power, a currency that's both potent and pervasive.

Now don't get me wrong. It's not all cloak and dagger. The partnership between MNCs and governments can also bear fruit in the form of economic development, innovation, and even environmental sustainability. However, the billion-dollar question (quite literally) is, whose interests are being served? The public's or the shareholders'? Spoiler alert: it's rarely the former.

The Dark Side of Diplomacy

Fancy a case study? Discussing the notorious banana war could be intriguing. No, this isn't a low-budget sci-fi flick; it's a real-life saga of how trade disputes can escalate into full-blown diplomatic crises. MNCs in the agribusiness sector literally redraw geopolitical alliances over...wait for it...bananas. If that doesn't convince you of the power these entities wield, I'm not sure what will.

And it's not just economic policy they're after. MNCs have a vested interest in shaping labor laws, environmental regulations, and yes, even military engagements. The rationale is simple: stability is good for business. Whether that stability comes at the expense of human rights, well, that's a footnote in most boardroom discussions.

Consider adding a hint of irony to this narrative, shall we? While MNCs flex their diplomatic muscles, they remain conspicuously aloof when it comes to taking responsibility for the consequences of their actions. Pollution, exploitation, tax evasion—these are mere externalities, byproducts of the relentless pursuit of profit.

But hey, not all is doom and gloom. There's a growing demand for corporate accountability, driven by consumers, activists, and even shareholders. The idea is not to dismantle the influence of MNCs but to ensure that it's wielded responsibly. Easier said than done, but hey, Rome wasn't built in a day.

So where do we go from here? For starters, transparency wouldn't hurt. Knowing who's lobbying whom, for what purpose, can shine a light on the shadowy corridors of power. Furthermore, strengthening international regulations on corporate conduct could level the playing field, ensuring that MNCs serve the interests of the many, not just the privileged few.

Overall, MNCs have become de facto diplomats, negotiating the terms of globalization in their favor. The implications for democracy, sovereignty, and global equality are profound and far-reaching. As the lines between economic might and political power continue to blur, the challenge lies in harnessing this influence for the greater good, rather than letting it become a tool for division and exploitation.

In the theater of global diplomacy, MNCs have secured front-row seats. Whether they play the part of hero or villain, however, remains to be seen. So keep the popcorn ready; the drama is far from over.

Chapter 11:
Cyber Diplomacy and Information Warfare

So, you've weathered the storm through ten chapters of diplomatic intrigue, backdoor deals, and the shadowy dance of power — welcome to the digital age with open arms and wary eyes. Cyber diplomacy and information warfare are redefining what it means to wage war and broker peace without a single shot being fired—sometimes. Picture a world where a teenager in their bedroom can potentially influence the outcome of an election thousands of miles away, or where state-sponsored hackers can plunge a city into darkness with a few keystrokes. That's not the setup for the latest spy thriller; it's the reality we're living in. The battleground has shifted from physical terrain to the vast expanses of cyberspace, where countries jostle for supremacy, not with tanks and missiles but with bots and malware. It's a realm where the art of diplomacy involves safeguarding your own digital secrets while smoothly navigating the murky waters of cyber espionage. The strategies? Think less James Bond and more Mr. Robot —but with the same amount of intrigue and double-dealing. It's a game where defense means not just protecting your digital borders but also ensuring that your narrative wins in the court of public opinion. And if you thought the traditional methods of warfare were complex, you ain't seen nothing yet. Welcome to a world where the pen and the keyboard might be mightier than the sword, but only if you know whose hands they're in.

The Emerging Battlefield: Cyberspace

Entering into the exciting realm of cyber diplomacy marks a new chapter in the art of negotiation. The emergence of the digital age has brought a new level of complexity and intrigue to the traditional practices of diplomacy, adding a cloak-and-dagger element that was previously unseen. Imagine a world where the pen and the sword are outdone by the keyboard and the code. Well, you don't really have to imagine; you're living in it.

Cyberspace has become the Wild West of international relations, a place where boundaries blur and the usual rules seem to apply only when convenient. Countries, like seasoned duelists, stand off at high noon, only their weapons are cyberattacks and their dueling grounds vast networks of information.

Consider this: a hacker sitting in a dimly lit room can cause more disruption than a group of diplomats at a negotiation table. With a few keystrokes, they can influence elections, pilfer sensitive data, and even cripple entire cities. The battleground has shifted, and the stakes are as high as ever.

It's a realm where anonymity reigns supreme. Attackers can mask their true origins, making retaliation a murky affair. This world is not for the faint-hearted. It's a game of cat and mouse, where the mouse can be a ghost and the cat has to hunt with a blindfold on.

However, take a deep breath and reflect on the irony, perhaps even find amusement in it. The very tools designed to connect us, to bring us closer together, are now being weaponized to drive wedges between nations. It's as if Prometheus gave us the fire, and we decided to play with it to see how much we can burn.

The reality, though, is no laughing matter. Critical infrastructure, from power grids to water supplies, is at risk. Cyber warriors can turn off lights in a city or disrupt hospitals with impunity. It's the kind of

The Dark Side of Diplomacy

stuff that might have seemed far-fetched in a spy novel, but it's the world we navigate today.

In the grand chessboard of geopolitics, cyberattacks are the rogue pawns that move unpredictably, challenging the conventional wisdom of international strategy. They're the jokers in the pack, capable of upsetting well-laid plans with an unpredictability that traditional diplomacy struggles to contain.

So what does this mean for the future of diplomacy? It means adaptation. It means that alongside the charming ambassadors and their polished rhetoric, we now need cyber experts capable of speaking the language of code as fluently as they do their native tongues.

Diplomacy in cyberspace is less about grand gestures and more about subtle maneuvers. It's about building firewalls as much as bridges. It's about cyber defenses and offense, and understanding that in the digital age, knowledge isn't just power; it's a weapon.

There's no sugarcoating it; mastering this digital battle necessitates a fresh skill set. Where yesterday's diplomats were fluent in conversation, today's emissaries must be adept in encryption and cybersecurity.

And yet amidst this shadowy skirmish in cyberspace, there's a silver lining. Just as cyberspace can be a battlefield, it also offers a platform for dialogue and cooperation. After all, cyber threats are a common enemy, one that doesn't respect national boundaries.

Thus, we see the emergence of cyber diplomacy as a beacon of hope. It's an attempt to foster collaboration in an area where cooperation is not just beneficial but vital. Countries are gradually realizing that to safeguard themselves, they need to work together, sharing intelligence and best practices.

This collective effort in the digital domain is a testament to the adaptability of diplomacy. It shows that even in the face of new challenges, the essence of diplomacy —the quest for a common ground— persists.

And so as we traverse this new digital landscape, we need to remember the ultimate goal of diplomacy in cyberspace: to secure a digital future where the bits and bytes that define our era serve to unite rather than divide. It's a lofty goal, sure, but in a world where reality often reads like science fiction, who's to say it's unachievable?

In conclusion, the emergence of cyberspace as a battlefield has undoubtedly complicated the arena of international relations. Yet it also presents an opportunity for innovation in diplomacy. As we move forward, the blend of traditional diplomatic strategies with cyber savvy could well be the key to navigating the tumultuous waters of the 21st century's geopolitical landscape.

Strategies and Defenses Against Cyber Manipulation

Well, spinning right off the last thrill ride and into the depths of cyber manipulation in diplomacy and information warfare, it feels like jumping from the frying pan into the digital inferno. But here's the kicker: we're not just going to cry over spilt milk. No, we're going to mop it up. How, you ask? Buckle down; it's going to be a wild ride—oh wait, I promised not to say that.

First off, forewarned is forearmed. The cornerstone of any defense strategy against cyber manipulation is awareness. It's the same old story: You can't fight what you can't see. And in the cyber realm, visibility is as tricky as trying to read a book in the dark. So illuminating these cyber threats becomes priority number uno. Cue the dramatic music.

But awareness alone is like shouting about the leak in the ship without plugging it. That's where cybersecurity hygiene comes into play. Think of it as brushing your teeth, but for your computers and networks. Regular updates, strong passwords, and the good old two-factor authentication are your best pals. They're the unsung heroes in this saga.

Now don't get too comfy just yet. Enter the gladiators of the digital arena—cybersecurity professionals. These are the folks who eat, sleep, and breathe codes and firewalls. Engaging a team of dedicated cybersecurity experts to defend against cyber manipulation is less of an option and more of a necessity nowadays. Like bringing a cannon to a knife fight.

Layered defense mechanisms are next. Imagine your network as a medieval castle. You wouldn't just rely on the outer wall, right? You'd have guards, towers, moats, the works. Similarly, in cyberspace, deploying multiple layers of security—firewalls, intrusion detection systems, encryption—creates a robust defense that's tough to crack.

But what's a castle without its loyal subjects? Same with cybersecurity: you need to cultivate a culture of security awareness among all users. Even the best defenses can crumble if someone inside the gate opens a malicious email. So regular training and drills are the order of the day, making each user a vigilant sentry.

On the flip side, we can't forget the power of alliances. In the battle against cyber manipulation, no nation is an island. Sharing insights, threat intelligence, and best practices with allies can amplify everyone's defense capabilities. Think of it like the Avengers, but instead of fighting Thanos, they're combatting cyber threats.

Legislation and regulation also play pivotal roles. Enacting laws that define and penalize cyber manipulation sets the legal groundwork for combating these threats. It's akin to setting rules for a duel: it clarifies what's off-limits and arms the victims with legal recourse.

However, amidst erecting digital fortresses and drafting cyber laws, it's crucial to not overlook the importance of diplomacy. Engaging in dialogue with other nations, even potential adversaries, can help establish norms and expectations in cyberspace. Sometimes, penning a treaty is mightier than the sword—or in this case, the keyboard.

Peering into the toolbox of specific defenses, artificial intelligence (AI) and machine learning stand out. These technologies can analyze patterns and predict potential attacks before they happen. It's like having a crystal ball but for cyber threats. However, deploying AI isn't without its pitfalls; the ethical implications and potential for misuse add layers of complexity.

Public-private partnerships also emerge as a critical strategy. The government and private sector joining forces can create a united front against cyber manipulation. It combines public authority with the innovation and agility of the private sector. Think of it as a dynamic duo, where each complements the strengths of the other.

Transparency and accountability mechanisms can't be overstated. When a breach occurs, timely disclosure allows for quicker responses and reduces damage. It's about being upfront, which, surprisingly, can restore public trust and deter future attackers who thrive on secrecy and fear.

Moving from defense to offense, cyber threat hunting is an active defense measure. Instead of waiting for alarms to ring, cybersecurity teams proactively search for lurking threats. It's like going on a cyber safari, but instead of lions, they're tracking down malware and intruders.

Finally, while we're maneuvering through the digital battlefield, it's crucial to safeguard the values we hold dear—freedom, privacy, and the open exchange of ideas. In the zeal to secure our networks, sacrificing our liberties would mean the manipulators have already won. Thus, striking a balance is not just advisable; it's imperative.

In wrapping up this expedition into the strategies and defenses against cyber manipulation, it's evident there's no silver bullet. The landscape is as dynamic as it is perilous. But with the right mix of vigilance, innovation, and cooperation, navigating these tumultuous waters becomes less about surviving and more about thriving. After all, the digital age is here to stay, and so are we, ready to face its challenges head-on with a sly smirk and a savvy mind.

Chapter 12:
Moving Forward: Diplomacy in the 21st Century

The game of diplomacy hasn't just evolved—it's been turned on its head, spun around, and sent careening down a hill at breakneck speed. Gone are the days when backroom deals and hushed conversations in smoky rooms could shape the fate of nations. No, my friends, we're in the era of tweets dictating policy, where a viral video can stir international incidents faster than a diplomat can say "retract that statement." In the labyrinth that is 21st-century diplomacy, innovations aren't just a neat addition; they're the lifeblood of surviving the next news cycle. We're talking about hybrid strategies where cyber diplomacy meets old-school charm offensives, and where the art of the deal requires mastering the blockchain and TikTok just as much as wining and dining at state dinners. Addressing the challenges of this uber-connected world means recognizing that the digital footprint of a nation's foreign policy is as critical as its carbon footprint. So as we march (or maybe scroll) forward, the diplomacy playbook isn't just being rewritten—it's being live-streamed, with the world keeping score in real-time. Buckle—er, embrace the change, because the future of global diplomacy is here, and it's anything but business as usual.

Innovations in Diplomatic Strategy

Embarking on the thrilling journey of modern diplomacy uncovers a universe where age-old trade routes have morphed into lightning-fast data streams, and ancient parchment treaties have evolved into cutting-edge blockchain contracts. Get ready to dive into an exhilarating world of innovation and global interconnectedness. The evolution isn't just technological; it's a profound transformation of how states interact, negotiate, and sometimes, snoop around each other's backyards.

Gone are the days when diplomacy meant stuffy rooms and endless rounds of formal talks. Today's diplomats are as likely to wield a Twitter account as they are a diplomatic passport. The digital age has democratized information, but don't be fooled —it's also a double-edged sword. While we can now rally international support with a viral hashtag, misinformation can just as easily send those efforts into a tailspin.

One of the stark innovations in diplomatic strategy has been the rise of 'soft power'—a term that sounds like a paradox but is anything but. It's the ability to influence through culture, education, and economic initiatives rather than through coercion or payment. Think of it as the diplomatic equivalent of persuading your neighbor to trim their hedge by inviting them to a fabulous garden party rather than throwing the hedge trimmer over the fence.

Another fascinating development is the concept of 'smart diplomacy.' This buzzword signifies the integration of technology into diplomatic efforts. Smart diplomacy leverages big data analytics, artificial intelligence, and social media to not only predict geopolitical shifts but also to craft more nuanced foreign policies.

The world stage has also welcomed non-state actors into the diplomatic soirée. Tech giants, NGOs, and even influential individuals navigate a parallel course alongside traditional state actors, wielding significant influence. It's as if the geopolitical chess game has introduced a set of new pieces with moves that we're all scrambling to understand.

Moreover, cybersecurity has transitioned from a niche concern to a cornerstone of national security. In a world where a hacker can do more damage than a battalion of soldiers, diplomacy has expanded to include cyber alliances, treaties, and, unavoidably, a bit of cyber espionage. The goal here isn't just defense but creating a shared space where the rules of the digital realm are respected and upheld.

In terms of conflict resolution, mediation has evolved beyond mere negotiation. Initiatives now often include peacebuilding strategies that incorporate local communities and utilize technology to foster transparency and accountability. It's akin to fixing a leaky faucet with a precise toolkit rather than just tightening the screws and hoping for the best.

Climate diplomacy has emerged as another critical area. As the planet warms, nations realize that environmental issues don't respect borders. Diplomacy now includes a shared understanding that sustainability isn't just a policy choice but a survival strategy. The Paris Agreement stands as a testament to this collective epiphany, though its implementation is a whole other kettle of fish.

The resurgence of city diplomacy is another trend to watch. Cities are increasingly bypassing national governments to make their own international agreements on everything from climate change to trade. Imagine the mayor of your town jet-setting around the globe, striking deals that put your little corner of the world on the map. Quirky, yes, but increasingly a reality.

Women in diplomacy have also marked a significant shift. With more women serving as diplomats and foreign affairs ministers, there's a noticeable change in how discussions are framed and resolutions sought. Gender equality in diplomacy isn't just about fairness; it's about bringing diverse perspectives to the table —perspectives that are vital in a multifaceted global landscape.

The Dark Side of Diplomacy

The blend of culture and diplomacy should not be disregarded. Cultural diplomacy now plays a crucial role in international relations, with countries using art, music, and literature to build bridges and soften hearts. If bombs are diplomacy by other means, then perhaps movies, paintings, and concerts are peacemaking by other means.

The introduction of digital diplomacy and virtual embassies breaks down geographical barriers, allowing for real-time communication and collaboration across continents. It's like having a diplomatic Swiss Army knife; versatile, efficient, and remarkably less likely to cause a diplomatic incident.

Looking forward, the use of predictive analytics in diplomacy hints at a future where diplomats might anticipate and mitigate crises before they escalate. Imagine if we could predict a conflict the same way we forecast the weather. A tad optimistic, maybe, but the potential is there.

Lastly, the ever-evolving landscape of international law as it tries to keep pace with these innovations presents both challenges and opportunities. As the rules of the game adapt, so too must the players, ensuring that actions on the world stage are not just strategic but also just.

In wrapping up this joyride through contemporary diplomatic strategy, it's clear the field is no longer just about treaties and statecraft. It's a vibrant tapestry of technology, culture, ethics, and human ingenuity. As we navigate this complex but fascinating terrain, one can't help but marvel at the resilience and adaptability of diplomacy. It's a testament to the fact that, irrespective of the era, our global interdependence demands cooperation, understanding, and, above all, innovative approaches to peace and prosperity.

Addressing the Challenges of a Connected World

In an era where a tweet can propel global markets into a frenzy and a hashtag can mobilize millions, the landscape of diplomacy has undergone seismic shifts. The connected world we live in now brings with it a unique blend of challenges and opportunities.

First off, the sheer speed at which information travels is staggering. Gone are the days when diplomatic cables were the primary source of communication. Today, a leader's offhand remark can become international news before their PR team has had their coffee. This instantaneous nature of communication places enormous pressure on diplomatic relations, necessitating a level of agility and savvy that was previously unrequired.

Then there's the issue of misinformation. In this golden age of connectivity, distinguishing truth from fiction can feel akin to finding a needle in a stack of needles. False narratives, deepfakes, and outright lies can spread with alarming speed, undermining trust and complicating diplomatic efforts. It's like trying to play chess on a board where half of the pieces are holograms.

Furthermore, the democratization of diplomacy through social media platforms has blurred the lines of official diplomatic channels. When every citizen with Internet access can engage in public diplomacy, it introduces a cacophony of voices into discussions that were once carefully curated. While this can amplify important messages, it also means that managing national narratives and fostering coherent international dialogues has become akin to herding cats.

The digital divide is another intriguing challenge to talk about. For all its perks, the connected world isn't equally accessible to all nations or individuals, exacerbating existing inequalities and creating new forms of digital colonialism. While some countries wield the Internet as a tool of power and influence, others find themselves on the outside looking in, struggling to have their voices heard amid the digital noise.

Data sovereignty has also emerged as a contentious issue. In an age where data is king, questions about who owns, controls, and has access to data have sparked international disputes. It's like a global game of keep-away but with higher stakes, touching on issues of privacy, security, and economic competitiveness.

The prevalence of cyber warfare adds yet another layer of complexity. States now wield the power to cripple each other's infrastructure, meddle in elections, and steal sensitive information without firing a single bullet. This shadowy battleground has necessitated new rules of engagement, with diplomats having to double as cyber warriors.

But it's not all doom and gloom. The connected world also offers unprecedented opportunities for diplomacy. Citizen diplomacy, for example, has been empowered by digital platforms, allowing individuals to engage in cultural exchanges and foster understanding in ways that were previously unimaginable.

Similarly, digital technologies have enabled diplomatic missions to become more transparent and accessible. Live-streamed negotiations and virtual town halls can help demystify the diplomatic process, building trust and facilitating greater public engagement.

The rise of digital diplomacy also allows for more efficient crisis response and humanitarian aid coordination. Social media platforms have been leveraged to organize evacuations, disseminate critical information during disasters, and galvanize global support for relief efforts.

Moreover, the international community has begun to address some of these challenges head-on. Task forces on misinformation, cybersecurity alliances, and global norms for state behavior in cyberspace are all steps in the right direction. It's a bit like assembling the Avengers, but instead of battling aliens, they're tackling deepfakes and data breaches.

Adapting to this new reality requires a radical rethinking of diplomatic training and education. Today's diplomats must be as comfortable navigating digital landscapes as they are in traditional negotiation settings. They need to become fluent in the language of memes and hashtags, understanding both their power and their peril.

One promising development is the growing collaboration between governments and tech companies. By working together, they can devise solutions to some of the thorniest issues at the intersection of technology and diplomacy. Think of it as a buddy cop movie, but instead of chasing down criminals, they're chasing down bots and trolls.

Finally, there's a need for a renewed emphasis on digital literacy and critical thinking among the general populace. In a world teeming with information, the ability to critically assess sources and resist manipulation is paramount. It's like developing a mental immune system to protect against the viruses of misinformation.

So while charting a course through the turbulent waters of the 21st century, it is crucial not to lose sight of the opportunities that this connected world presents . Yes, the challenges are daunting, but with creativity, collaboration, and a dash of humor, we can navigate this digital age with finesse. After all, if we managed to turn cat videos into a global phenomenon, surely we can harness the power of connectivity for the greater good of diplomacy, right?

Addressing the challenges of a connected world is akin to solving a Rubik's Cube while riding a roller coaster — it's complex and disorienting, but ultimately solvable with patience, skill, and a bit of luck. As we move forward, let's embrace both the chaos and the potential, crafting a diplomatic landscape that leverages the best of what technology has to offer while mitigating its pitfalls.

Chapter 13:
Shaping a More Transparent Future for Diplomacy

So we've traipsed through the shadowed alleys of diplomacy, peeking behind those gilded curtains to catch glimpses of the puppeteers. It's been quite the expedition, hasn't it? We've navigated the murky waters where sharks of statecraft swim, witnessed the artful dodgers of diplomacy at play, and even gotten our hands a little dirty in the cyber dust of information warfare. Now as our soiree in the dimly lit corridors of global maneuvering winds down, it's time to ask: What comes next? How do we haul diplomacy into the glaring sunshine of the 21st century?

First off, we will hash out the obvious. Transparency in diplomacy isn't just a lofty ideal we're chasing after for kicks; it's a necessity for a more peaceful, fair, and, dare I say, less Kafkaesque world order. The days of smoke-filled rooms where the fate of millions is decided should be booted out the window. And yes, that includes even those e-cig vape clouds some of our modern negotiators are so fond of. It's time for the cards to be laid out on the table.

Imagine a world where diplomatic agreements aren't shrouded in secrecy but are live-streamed. A tad radical? Perhaps. But consider the upside: accountability. When diplomats know the world's watching, the incentive to wheel and deal under the table diminishes. There's nothing like the disinfectant of sunlight to clean out the murky underbelly of international relations.

Now on to the elephant in the room—the digital era. Cyber diplomacy and information warfare have turned the once staid field of diplomacy into something akin to a hacker's wet dream. The digital frontier is the new battleground, and it's about time our diplomatic endeavors caught up. Ensuring secure, transparent channels for digital diplomacy isn't just good sense; it's self-preservation.

But wait, there's more. We've seen the rise of non-state actors and multinational conglomerates that hold sway over international policies. These entities, often operating in the shadows, have the power to influence global politics, often bypassing traditional diplomatic channels. Incorporating these actors into a transparent system of diplomacy is crucial. It's high time these shadow players were brought into the light, making them part of the solution rather than letting them remain part of the problem.

Don't get me wrong; the call for transparency isn't about airing dirty laundry for the sake of scandal. It's about building trust. The shenanigans we've seen, the covert operations, the economic under-the-table nudges—they've created a world where suspicion is the norm. By fostering transparency, we're not just clearing the air; we're restructuring how trust is built on the global stage.

How do we achieve this, you ask? It starts with policy—laws and regulations that mandate transparency in diplomatic negotiations and dealings. But it's more than just rules and regulations; it's about fostering a diplomatic culture that values openness. The shift won't be overnight, and it won't be easy. It requires rethinking the very foundation of diplomacy.

This call to action isn't a solo mission. It requires concerted effort from nations, NGOs, civil societies, and, yes, even the very individuals who revel in the shadows of old-school diplomacy. It's about legacy—what kind of world do we want to leave behind? One shrouded in se-

The Dark Side of Diplomacy

crecy, or one where openness paves the way for a more equitable world?

Detractors might argue that some level of secrecy is essential for national security or for delicate negotiations. Sure, not every diplomatic discussion can be an open book. However, the default setting should lean toward openness, with secrecy being the exception, not the rule. It's about finding the right balance.

And in the spirit of putting our money where our mouth is, this push for transparency also needs to extend to the economic levers of diplomacy. Economic sanctions, trade agreements, aid—all these tools that nations wield in the arena of international relations should come with a hefty dose of transparency. Who's making the deals, under what conditions, and with what expected outcomes?

As for the role of technology, it's a double-edged sword. While it facilitates the obfuscation of true diplomatic intentions, it also offers unprecedented tools for transparency. Blockchain, anyone? Imagine a world where diplomatic agreements and treaties are recorded in an immutable ledger, accessible to all. It's not just about preventing tampering; it's about fostering trust through verifiable transparency.

Of course, none of this means anything without the watchdogs—the press, the whistleblowers, the civic activists. These guardians of the public interest play a crucial role in holding the diplomatic process accountable. Their access to information should not only be protected but expanded. After all, sunlight is the best disinfectant.

A more transparent future for diplomacy isn't just a pipe dream; it's a possibility, grounded in the realities of our interconnected, digital world. It's a call to arms, or rather, a call to disarm the shadows. We've seen the alternative—a world mired in suspicion, covert operations, and backroom deals. Isn't it time we chose a different path?

So as we close the cover on this voyage through the murky guises of diplomacy, remember the trip on which we have embarked. Shaping a transparent future for diplomacy isn't just wishful thinking; it's a necessity. A call to light the beacons, if you will, and ensure that the future of international relations is not decided in the dark.

The road ahead is fraught with challenges, no doubt. Yet history demonstrates that change is achievable through tenacity, vision, and, yes, a smidgeon of idealism. Avoid shying away from reimagining diplomacy for the 21st century—a diplomacy that is open, transparent, and accountable. The world deserves no less, and frankly, it's about time.

Appendix

Here we are, at the tail end of our whirlwind tour through the shadowy hallways of global diplomacy. If you've made it this far without developing a slight sense of paranoia or an overwhelming urge to dive into a rabbit hole of political intrigue documentaries, then my hat's off to you. Let's talk a bit about why this little section exists, shall we?

The journey through the dark side of diplomacy isn't for the faint of heart. It's a blend of high stakes poker, three-dimensional chess, and, oddly enough, a soap opera. It's got its heroes, villains, and those who are too complex to neatly fit into either category. Given the roller coaster we've been on, you might be wondering—what's left to say?

Well, this appendix isn't just a catch-all for the tidbits that didn't make it into the main act. Think of it as the bonus track of an album: not necessary for the story's progression but enriching to the experience. Here, I've gathered a collection of additional insights, resources, and reflections to aid you, the astute explorer, in navigating the labyrinthian world of politics.

Historical Dark Side of Diplomacy

Diplomatic Intrigue: A Saga of Deception and Betrayal Through the Ages

A History of Deception and Betrayal Diplomacy

A drama of the ages played out on the stage of diplomatic intrigue: a world where the destinies of nations and dynasties were determined by the decisions of a few, where the competition for power and prestige was a backdrop for the novels of the past; the setting in which people like to believe that events were shaped and bent by individuals who could be decided on a whim.

Imagine a world where the destiny of nations was played out by the intrigue of diplomats, where the desire to enhance prestige and power struggles always set the scene for gripping historical events. Yes, welcome to the world of diplomatic maneuvering, where the veneer of civility frequently masked the undercurrents of duplicity and deception. Come with me on this journey to examine some of the greatest feats of diplomatic legerdemain in the history of the planet.

In 1494, the Treaty of Tordesillas paved the way for a major fraud. The Church gave Spain and Portugal carte blanche to divide up the world between them, riding roughshod over the rights of those displaced from their lands. This act of colonial hubris would plant the seeds of later struggles for freedom and independence. Fast forward a few centuries to the 19th century, and the scene was just as intriguing. When the Congress of Vienna met, monarchs gathered to reestablish equilibrium in Europe, dividing nations as if in a coin toss. Poland was "partitioned," Norway was "ceded" to Sweden, and the German states were "assigned" to Austria. This peace, if it can be called that, followed two centuries of endless little wars, which occasionally culminated in a major war or a world compromise. However, the threshold of a large "general" war had once and for all proved to be too dangerous for modern European states.

The 19th century saw an even bolder play, unprecedented in the history of diplomacy. Unable to stem the tide of imports, China attempted to ban foreign goods, which only resulted in the British smuggling opium into the country and getting the whole nation addicted. With the British East India Company exploiting their military superiority, the Treaty of Nanking was dictated in 1842, demonstrating that power was now trumped by self-interest.

The assassination of Archduke Franz Ferdinand in 1914 showed how intricate treaties, arms races, and espionage could explode into a world catastrophe, leading to the First World War. The war was the result of a fragile web of secret agreements and deals. One example of this fragility was the Zimmermann Telegram, a German effort to ally with Mexico against the US. This telegram was intercepted and decrypted, pushing the US into the war. The reverberations of diplomatic treachery through the ages even survived the aftermath of the Great War.

One of the most influential geopolitical events of the 20th century was the Sykes-Picot Agreement of 1916. This clandestine agreement not only disassembled the Ottoman Empire but also divided its lands among the British and French, neither of whom cared about the people who lived there or their ethnic, religious, and tribal identities. The result was decades of chaos and violence that swept the region. Imperial hubris often has a disastrous legacy. Both the Munich Agreement of 1938, where appeasement by Chamberlain convinced Hitler he could push ahead, and the Molotov-Ribbentrop Pact of 1939, which decisively rerouted the Second World War, serve as sharp reminders of the promise and peril of diplomacy.

Our story ends with the 1945 Yalta Conference, which brings a bitter aftertaste. While the West claimed to uphold democratic principles worldwide, its leaders had no problem with the Soviet Union getting its way in Eastern Europe, starting what would become known as the Cold War. This period, in practice, was one of the most violent eras in human history.

These are tales of diplomatic double-cross, chicanery, and treachery, and a warning that all is not what it seems in the looking-glass world of diplomacy. They illustrate the persistence of ambition, the perils of shortsightedness, and the potential for cooperation and betrayal that is always within us. As we know, it is history repeating itself in stasis while we watch.

Why This Matters

In the grand scheme of things, understanding the undercurrents of global power isn't just about stocking up on interesting party conversation. It's about recognizing the forces shaping our world. As citizens of this increasingly interconnected global village, the more we know, the better equipped we are to advocate for the future we want to see. Plus, let's be honest: Untangling the web of international intrigue is about as exhilarating as it gets.

Further Reading and Resources

For those hungry for more, I encourage diving into the oceans of literature that expand on the topics we've covered. From the art of negotiation to the mechanics of multinational corporations, there's a world of knowledge waiting for you. Explore your local library, scour the Internet, and immerse yourself in the fascinating, if sometimes maddening, world of international relations.

A Final Note

In conclusion, always remember that the realm of politics and diplomacy is not just the domain of statesmen and secret agents. It's a space where each of us has a role to play, whether we're casting our vote, engaging in spirited debates with friends, or simply staying informed about the world around us. As you close this book (figuratively, because let's face it, you're probably reading this on some sort of electronic device), carry with you not just the knowledge of how the world works but the resolve to make it better.

The Dark Side of Diplomacy

And if all else fails, remember this: The world of diplomacy might be complex, but it's also endlessly fascinating. May your journey through it be as enlightening as it is entertaining. Until next time.

Glossary of Terms

As we navigate the intricate world of global politics and the nuanced practices of diplomacy, it's essential to familiarize ourselves with specific terms that frequently emerge. This glossary serves as a comprehensive guide to understanding key concepts discussed throughout this book. It's designed to enrich the reader's comprehension and foster a deeper insight into the complexities of international relations.

Arbitration

An international conflict resolution method where a neutral third party provides a binding decision on a dispute between two nations, often utilized to avoid the escalation of conflicts and maintain diplomatic relations.

Coercion

The act of compelling a party to act in an involuntary manner by use of threats, sanctions, or some other form of pressure. Within the realm of diplomacy, coercion is a tactic used to influence the decision-making and behavior of states or non-state actors.

Diplomatic Immunity

A privilege granted to diplomats and their families, which exempts them from the jurisdiction of the host country's laws. This immunity ensures that diplomats can perform their duties without fear of harassment or arrest.

Geopolitics

The study of how geographic location and natural resources influence political power and international relations. Geopolitics often plays a crucial role in shaping nations' foreign policies and strategic decisions.

Information Warfare

The use and manipulation of information to gain a competitive advantage, often through means such as misinformation, disinformation, and cyber attacks. Information warfare aims to undermine the opponent's position without direct confrontation.

Multilateralism

An approach to international relations in which multiple countries work together on a given issue. Multilateralism is characterized by diplomatic alliances, treaties, and international organizations that aim to address global challenges collectively.

Non-State Actors

Entities that participate in international relations and have significant influence but do not represent a government or state. Examples include NGOs, multinational corporations, and terrorist groups.

Proxy War

A conflict where two opposing states or entities support combatants that serve their interests instead of waging war directly. Proxy wars have been a prevalent strategy during the Cold War and continue to shape international relations.

Sanctions

Restrictive measures imposed by one or more countries onto others to pressure change in policy or conduct. Sanctions can be economic, diplomatic, or military and often aim to isolate the target country to force compliance with international laws or norms.

Soft Power

The ability of a country to persuade or attract others to do what it wants without force or coercion. Soft power relies on cultural or ideological appeal, diplomacy, and economic influence.

Sovereignty

The full right and power of a governing body to govern itself without any interference from outside sources or bodies. In international law, sovereignty is a key principle that underpins the international system of states.

Statecraft

The art of managing state affairs, which includes the development and execution of foreign policy. Statecraft involves a comprehensive understanding of both the domestic and international political landscape to advance national interests.

Supranational Organization

An entity created by multiple nations to pursue goals that are beyond the scope or capability of any single nation. Such organizations hold authority that can supersede national governments, with the European Union being a prime example.

With this glossary, readers should now have a better understanding of the unique terminology used when discussing the dynamic field of international politics and diplomacy. As we venture deeper into the geopolitical landscape, these terms will serve as essential tools for analysis and discussion.

List of Acronyms

In the intricate world of international politics, acronyms often serve as shorthand for the complex entities and concepts that shape global relations. This section aims to demystify the alphabet soup that readers will encounter throughout this book. Understanding these acronyms will not only enhance comprehension but also enrich the reader's engagement with the material. Here's a concise overview of key acronyms pertinent to the discussion on diplomacy, geopolitics, and the mechanisms of power.

UN - United Nations: A cornerstone of international diplomacy, the UN plays a central role in maintaining peace, security, and fostering global cooperation.

NATO - North Atlantic Treaty Organization: A military alliance established in 1949, encompassing North American and European countries for mutual defense against aggression.

EU - European Union: A political and economic union of 27 European countries that are tied by an internal single market and a standardized set of laws.

WTO - World Trade Organization: An intergovernmental organization regulating international trade by providing a framework for negotiating trade agreements and settling disputes.

NGO - Non-Governmental Organization: Non-profit groups that operate independently of any government, typically aiming to address social, political, or environmental issues.

MNC - Multinational Corporation: Companies that produce and sell goods or services in multiple countries outside of their home country.

CIA - Central Intelligence Agency: A civilian foreign intelligence service of the federal government of the United States, tasked with gathering, processing, and analyzing national security information.

NSA - National Security Agency: A national-level intelligence agency of the United States Department of Defense, responsible for global monitoring, collection, and processing of information and data for foreign intelligence and counterintelligence purposes.

BRICS - Brazil, Russia, India, China, and South Africa: An acronym for an association of five major emerging national economies that collaborate on issues related to economic development and global governance.

ISIS - Islamic State of Iraq and Syria: A terrorist organization that follows a fundamentalist, Wahhabi doctrine of Sunni Islam.

As we navigate the labyrinthine paths of diplomatic maneuvering, these acronyms will often light our way, offering concise keys to understanding the broad spectrum of players and principles at work. Armed with this knowledge, readers are better equipped to grasp the subtleties and complexities of global diplomacy.

Recommended Resources

So, you've meandered through the winding alleys of diplomacy's underbelly, and you're hungry for more? Good. It's about time we rolled up our sleeves and dove headfirst into some resources that'll sharpen your insights further. These aren't your run-of-the-mill, dry academic texts that'll put you to sleep faster than a diplomat's monologue. Nope. They're more like the cheat codes to understanding the Machiavellian maneuvers in the global political arena.

The Dark Side of Diplomacy

- **"The Prince" by Machiavelli** - Okay, let's get the obvious out of the way. If you haven't yet, you've got to crack open this bad boy. It's practically the OG playbook for power tactics and realpolitik. Sure, it's from the Renaissance, but you'd be surprised how its cunning counsel on leadership and manipulation gives you X-ray vision into today's political shenanigans.

- **"Confessions of an Economic Hit Man" by John Perkins** - If you thought our chapter on economic hit men was a wild ride, Perkins' firsthand account will make your jaw drop. It's part tell-all memoir, part exposé, revealing the gritty reality of how economic pressure is used as a weapon. After diving into this, you won't look at international loans and aid the same way again.

- **"The Shock Doctrine" by Naomi Klein** - For a deep dive into how crises are exploited to push radical economic policies, Klein's masterpiece is a must-read. It's a riveting tale of "disaster capitalism," showing you the playbook some wield to reshape economies in the wake of upheavals. You'll start to see the patterns and, maybe, predict the next moves on the global stage.

- **"By Way of Deception" by Victor Ostrovsky** - A gripping memoir revealing the inner workings of Mossad, Israel's intelligence agency, and its controversial operations. Ostrovsky exposes clandestine missions, ethical dilemmas, and the agency's secretive culture, offering a revealing insight into one of the world's most renowned intelligence organizations.

- **"The Other Side Of Deception" by Victor Ostrovsky** - Delves further into the covert world of Mossad, shedding light on its deceptive strategies and controversial operations. Through firsthand accounts, Ostrovsky exposes the agency's manipulation of information and international affairs, offering a provocative exploration of espionage and its moral complexities.

- **"White Malice: The CIA and the Covert Recolonization of Africa" by Dr. Susan Williams** - a groundbreaking examination of the CIA's clandestine activities in Africa, revealing its role in perpetuating instability and undermining African sovereignty. Through meticulous research and compelling narratives, Dr. Williams exposes the hidden agendas behind American interventions, offering a critical analysis of neocolonialism and its impact on the continent.

Each of these reads packs a punch in its own right, blending insights with intrigue. They don't just inform; they inspire you to look deeper, question more, and, perhaps, decode the next big political move before it hits the headlines. So grab a coffee, or something stronger (you might need it), and plunge into these pages. Who knows? You might just be the next armchair analyst uncovering the hidden forces shaping our world.